WALKS AND SCRAMBLES

IN THE JULIAN ALPS

BASED ON KRANJSKA GORA

BY MIKE NEWBURY

ZLATOROG PUBLICATIONS

This book is dedicated to

Dušan Polajnar

Steadfast Mountain Guide

Acknowledgements:
The author would like to thank all his helpers, especially
Pat Newbury, and Jimmy Smith of West Lothian;
and record his appreciation of the many Slovenians who
set him on his way.

Copyright © Mike Newbury 2003
Zlatorog Publications
The Old Granary, West Mill St., Perth PH1 5QP

Printed by
Lothian Print, Edinburgh
Graphics by Tom Prentice, Glasgow

Reprinted with minor revisions November 2006

ISBN 9780954522704

CONTENTS

	page
INTRODUCTION: **THE MOUNTAINS OF ENCHANTMENT**	7
SLOVENIAN PRACTICALITIES	12

1. Travel and accommodation
2. Currency and prices
3. Local transport
   (1) Buses
   (2) Taxis
   (3) Cycle hire
   (4) Car hire
   (5) Lifts
4. Language
5. The huts
6. Summer weather in the Julians
7. The dangers and how to minimise them
8. Techniques for 'equipped' routes (via ferrata)
9. Maps required
10. Local guides
11. Estimates of time and effort

THE ROUTES   25

1. Mainly downhill from Vršič   25
   (1) To Trenta
   (2) To Trenta via the traverse
   (3) To Kranjska Gora
   (4) To Tamar and Rateče via the Sleme saddle

2. Mala Mojstrovka: the traverse from the north   32

3. Jalovec: the traverse from Tamar to Vršič   34

4. South from Trenta   36
   (1) By the Seven Lakes Valley to Bohinj
   (2) Variants:
      (i) Alternative route from Trenta to Prehodavci
      (ii) The Špičje ridge
      (iii) The Tičarica - Zelnarica ridge
      (iv) Prehodavci to Dolič by Hribarice
      (v) Prehodavci to Dolič by the north wall of Kanjavec

5. Prisojnik (Prisank)   42
  (1) The traverse through the Windows
  (2) The south side:
    (i) Past the Great Window
    (ii) To the saddle of Zadnji Prisojnik
    (iii) The South gully
  (3) The Hanzova pot

6. Špik: The ascent from Krnica   53

7. Kriški podi   55
  (1) The traverse from Krnica to Trenta
  (2) Variants:
    (i) Over Razor to Vršič
    (ii) To Škrlatica and Vrata
    (iii) Over Križ, Stenar and Bovški Gamsovec to Luknja

8. Triglav by the northern approaches   61
  (1) The Plemenice Route and the South ridge to the Summit.
  (2) The Prag Route and the East ridge to the summit
  (3) The Tominškova Route
  (4) Deviations from the Staničev Hut: the ascent of Rjavina

ENVOI   70

SKETCH MAPS AND DIAGRAMS

Guidebook Area   8

Kranjska Gora   11

Vršič Area   24

West of Vršič   26

Trenta to Bohinj   37

Prisojnik Area   43

Prisojnik Summit   45

Kriški Podi   56

Triglav - Northern Approaches   62

PHOTOGRAPHS photo pages

Photo number
1. View of Razor (left) and Prisojnik from Hotel Lek   i
2. Kranjska Gora - village centre
3. Looking south over Kranjska Gora to Prisojnik
                                                                    ii
4. Above Trenta (Route 1(1))
5. Tourists approaching Soča Source
6. Old road from Vršič (Route 1(3))
7. Prisojnik from Poštarska Hut (Route 1(3)) (Devil's pillar centre right)
                                                                    iii
8. Mala Mojstrovka from Vratica saddle (Route 1(4) and Route 2)
9. Jalovec from Sleme saddle (Route 1(4))
10. Descending the Črna voda ravine (Route 1(4))
11. Tamar Hut and Jalovec (Route 1(4) and Route 3)
                                                                    iv
12. The path from Tamar (Route 1(4))
13. Looking towards Vratica from Route 2
14. Ascent of Mala Mojstrovka (Route 2) (Climber: Barrie Brown)
15. Summit of Mala Mojstrovka from top of crag (Route 2)
16. Stone chute on Mala Mojstrovka from Vršič (Route 2)
17. Špička Hut on Jalovec (Route 3)
                                                                    v
18. Jalovec from southeast (Špička Hut below rock cone on left) (Route 1(2) & 3)
19. Jalovec - summit ridge (Route 3)
20. Path down towards Špička Hut (Route 3)
                                                                    vi
21. Prehodavci Hut (Vršac on left, Kanjavec on right) (Route 4)
22. Špičje ridge from near Triglav Lakes Hut (Route 4(1))
23. The Prehodavci - Dolič traverse (Route 4(2)(v))
                                                                    vii
24. Prisojnik: start of equipped sections of Route 5(1)
25. The first steep section of Route 5(1)
26. The maiden's face from Route 5(1)

5

photo pages

27. The crux of the ascent (Route 5(1))
28. Climbing the bulge on the crux (Route 5(1))
29. The Great Window of Prisojnik from the road
30. Approaching the Window (Route 5(1))
31. Climbing up to the Window
*32. Looking down through the Window
   (Here Route 5(2)(i) joins 5(1) to the summit)*

33. Summit of Prisojnik from the west (Route 5(1) and Route 5(2)(i))
34. Razor and Triglav from summit of Prisojnik
35. Approaching the East Window (Route 5(1))

36. Škrlatica group and Špik from Gozd Martuljek
37. Ascending Kriška Stena (Routes 7)
38. Ascending Kriška stena in mist (Routes 7)
39. Pogačnikov Hut from Bovška vratica (Routes 7)

40. Triglav from Partizans Memorial at Vrata (Routes 8)
41. Cmir from above Kredarica
42. Mali Triglav and Kredarica Hut from summit of Triglav (Route 8(2))
43. Tominškova (Route 8(3)) looking back to saddle at start of equipped section

44. On Tominškova (Route 8(3))
45. On Tominškova (Route 8(3))
46. The Prag (Route 8(2))
47. Approaching the summit ridge of Rjavina (Route 8(4))
48. The step on the ridge of Rjavina (Route 8(4)) (Climber: Dušan Polajnar)
49. Triglav from Rjavina (Route 8(4))

Note
Some captions on the photographs are shortened from the foregoing

Front cover: *Jalovec from the Sleme saddle*
Back cover: *Approaching Mala Mojstrovka from Vratica*

All photographs by the Author

INTRODUCTION:
THE MOUNTAINS OF ENCHANTMENT

The Slovenian Julians form an intricate group of jagged limestone peaks penetrated by deep forested valleys. At their heart rises Triglav (2864m.), the national symbol of Slovenia. Named after a three-headed deity, Triglav ('v' pronounced 'w') is celebrated in legend and has inspired poets and composers. It is also at the core of the unspoilt Triglav National Park.

"Triglav reigns over a dreamworld sundered from time, full of unbelievable hidden nooks, of unsuspected passages, of sudden visions of cliffs which cannot be real. Surely there is no other mountain land like this." (Tom Longstaff, writing to Julius Kugy).

Every year I have been privileged to wander alone out of the wild forest and up the limestone rock walls, their ledges jewelled with alpine flowers. I use marked routes with fixed rungs and cables which would be anathema here, but which are almost invisible in the vast crags.

By Alpine standards, the height of the main peaks is modest: Triglav (2864m.) down to Mala Mojstrovka (2332m.). ('j' pronounced 'y', 'v' pronounced 'w'). With a start from (say) Kranjska Gora at 810m., that provides ascents of 1500-2000m. so that the scale is generally about twice that of Scottish hills unless starting from a hut or from Vršič pass.

Up to about 1600m, the mountains are clothed in natural forest, mostly beech and spruce, but steep slopes and crags continue down through the forest into ravines: in the area of this guide book, only the main east-west valley past Kranjska Gora and the valleys south from that village and from Rateče (the accent imports an 'h' in Slovene pronunciation) have fairly level floors, with here and there, open meadows. At the top of the forest, the natural sequence of vegetation provides a shrubby zone (whose equivalent is almost eliminated from Britain) dominated by scattered larches and thickets of dwarf pine.

Small flocks of sheep and a few cattle wander around the top of the forests, and chamois and ibex may be seen on remote crags and pastures, but compared to Britain, the grazing and browsing is minimal, and the

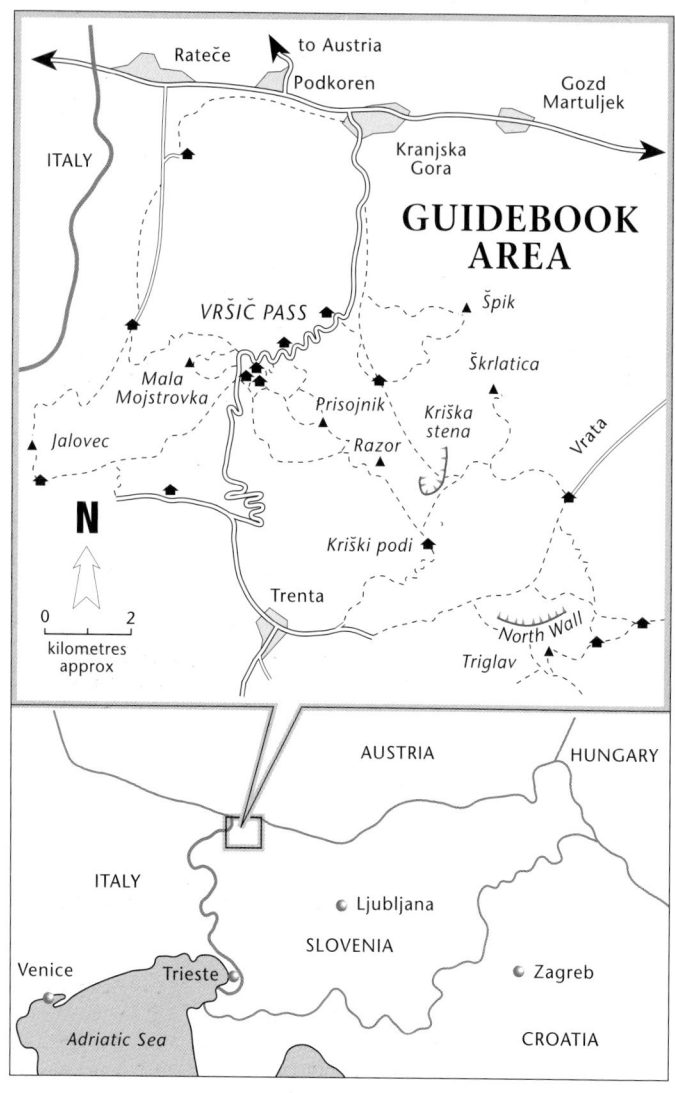

free draining lime-rich soils produce an astounding array of wild flowers. Even the non-botanist may enjoy the varieties of gentians, harebells and saxifrages flourishing on the crags, the cushions of the pink Triglav rose (potentilla nitida) near the summits and the dwarf yellow and white poppies blooming alone in wastes of scree.

Insects are mercifully few but so are wild birds, apart from swallows and martins near the villages and the acrobatic choughs looking for food scraps at the summit cairns.

The area of this guidebook is bounded on the north by the road from the Italian border eastwards towards Ljubljana (capital of Slovenia) past the villages of Rateče, Podkoren, Kranjska Gora, Gozd Martuljek and Mojstrana.

On the west side, a road runs southwards from Rateče near the Italian border up the Planica valley to terminate at the Tamar Hut below Jalovec. On the east a road runs south from Mojstrana ('Moystrana') to terminate at the Vrata Hut (Aljažev dom) at the foot of Triglav; and from Kranjska Gora (810m.) in the middle runs the only road over the Slovenian Julians, namely over the pass of Vršič (1611m.) to the deep Trenta Valley. This provides a useful high start for the mountains on either side as well as for excellent mainly downhill routes.

Alpine huts (denoted 'dom' or 'koča') provide overnight accommodation, drinks and simple meals (see below).

The whole area apart from the village of Kranjska Gora and a strip immediately east and west of it, is within the protected Triglav National Park, with restrictions on wild camping, off-road cycling and such activities as plant collecting.

NOTE 1

The principal routes described here are all shown on the maps, and they are waymarked, with a single exception (the old grassed road from Vršič towards Kranjska Gora).

I have done them all personally, some many times, but the amount of detail I noted or remember varies, and consequently, a few of the route descriptions are sparse. I regret that uncertainty of re-inspection makes it unwise to hold back on that account. There are a few marked routes accessible from Kranjska Gora which I have not done and these are indicated separately as possibilities. Any significant adjustments or additions which readers would like me to make will be considered for publication (with acknowledgement) in any future edition of this guidebook.

I have endeavoured to be accurate, but cannot guarantee that there are no mistakes; also, routes are liable to damage and change; and whilst I have warned of various dangers, not all can be foreseen. I therefore take no responsibility for accidents or mishaps befalling users of this guidebook.

NOTE 2

It is not always fully appreciated in this country that Slovenia has been independent since 1991. After brief independence in the 9th century, Slovenia was under foreign domination until 1918, but the Slovenes maintained a powerful cultural identity. After World War I under the Kingdom of Serbs, Croats and Slovenes and after World War II under the Republic of Yugoslavia, Slovenes suffered the perceived domination of the Serbs. Occupying the most prosperous and advanced part of Yugoslavia, they believed that they were subsidising the rest. The first free elections in Yugoslavia were held in Slovenia in April 1990 signalling the end of Communist rule. Following increasing tension, 88 per cent of the electorate voted for independence in December 1990. Negotiations with Belgrade proved abortive in face of the intransigence of Slobodan Milosovec, and despite attempts by Britain and others to preserve Yugoslavia as a federation, Slovenia declared independence on 25 June 1991. The Yugoslav invasion two days later disintegrated against unexpectedly powerful Slovene resistance and after a 10-day war, a truce was called followed by the withdrawal of Yugoslav forces. The EC finally recognised Slovenia in December 1991 and in May 1992, Slovenia was admitted to the United Nations. Slovenia became a member of the EU on 1 May 2004.

(For a fuller history of Slovenia and other general information, see the 'Lonely Planet' guidebook 'Slovenia' by Steve Fallon: ISBN 086442 538 4).

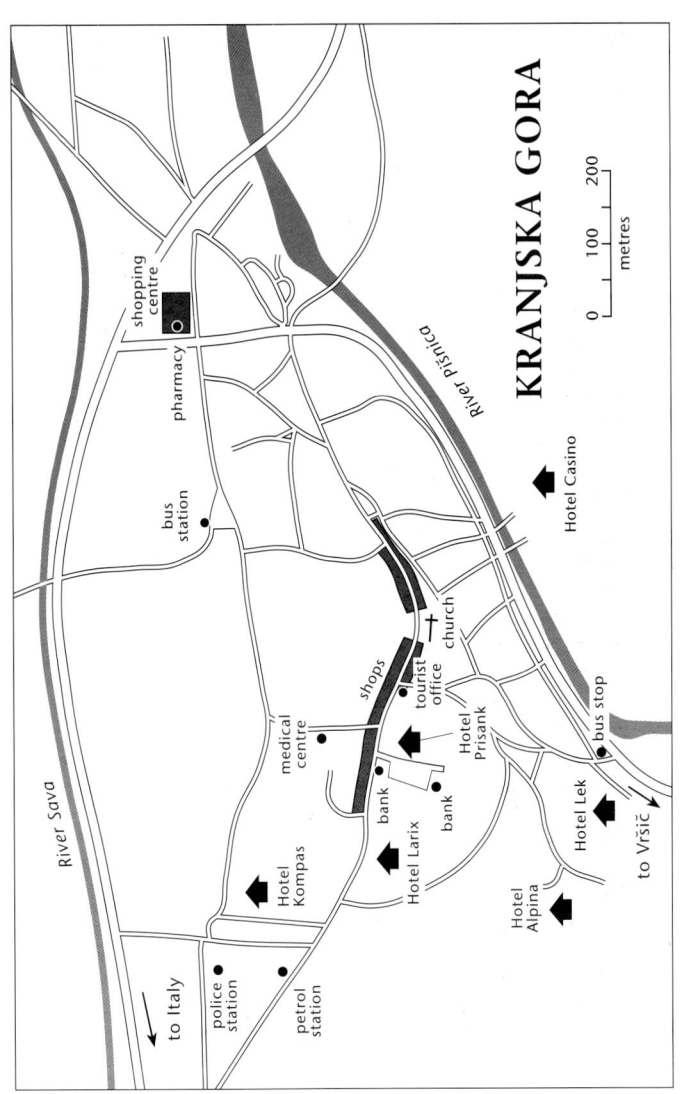

SLOVENIAN PRACTICALITIES

1. TRAVEL & ACCOMMODATION

Flights: There are many ways of flying to Slovenia. Here are several:-

Adria Airways (0207734 4630) the excellent Slovenian national airline, have flights to Ljubljana Airport from Gatwick, Birmingham and Dublin (as at 2006). Adria do not (2006) fly from Scotland; but, from Edinburgh, you can book a through ticket to Ljubljana via Prague with **Czech Airlines** (0870 444 3747), or via Paris with **Air France** (0870 142 4343) or via Frankfurt with **Lufthansa** (0870 837 7747). All these can of course be booked online, but a travel agent should find the cheapest suitable.

Flights to Salzburg in Austria involve about 4 hours transit through 7 tunnels on often congested roads.

Transit: From Brnik (Ljubljana airport) to Kranjska Gora takes about 45 minutes direct. Over the years I have had good and reliable service from the local taxi/minibus operator:-
Mitja Mertelj, Podkoren 73, 4280 Kranjska Gora.
Tel: 588 1655 (phoning from Britain prefix 003864 before 588).
Fax: 588 1655, e-mail: mitja.mertelj@telemach.net

Other operators can be found through the UK Slovenia Tourist Office or the Tourist Information Centre at Kranjska Gora (see below).

Accommodation: Self-catering accommodation in Kranjska Gora is plentiful, and modestly priced according to 'star' rating. You can buy mini-supermarket food for snacks, and eat out at one of a number of excellent establishments.

There are also guest-houses and hotels.

There is a well-appointed camp site at Gozd Martulek, 4km. along the main bus route towards Ljubljana.

Taking a package holiday using the same scheduled airlines and local hotels, is the simplest procedure.

Facilities include the pharmacy (in the shopping block beyond the bus station) and the medical centre (situated a few metres down from the village centre on the north side). Medical treatment is free apart from a very small administration charge: you will need to have your passport, and have the relevant page photo-copied at the post office. Public conveniences: no problem using hotel facilities!

Further information may be obtained from:

UK Slovenia Tourist Office
South Marlands,
Itchingfield
Horsham
West Sussex
RH13 0NN
Tel: 0870 225 5305   Fax: 0208 584 2017
e-mail: slovenia.tourism@virgin.net
www.slovenia.info

TIC Kranjska Gora
Tičarjeva 2 SI-4280 Kranjska Gora
Tel: 00386 4 580 9440   Fax: 00386 4 580 9441
e-mail: info@kranjska-gora.eu
www.kranjska-gora.si
They will provide a booklet showing local facilities and a list of accommodation.

2. CURRENCY AND PRICES

As from 1 January, 2007, the Slovenian currency is the Euro, easily obtainable at one of the two Kranjska Gora banks by using an appropriate card at their 'hole-in-the-wall' (instructions appear in English). Exchange is also available at some local hotels and at the Tourist Information Centre.

As at 2006 prices and exchange rates, basics are very cheap: a good evening meal with wine and coffee costs £7 - £10; good coffee about 70p., a half-litre of lager beer £1.20 - £1.30: and supermarket Slovenian wine £1.50 - £2.50 per litre bottle. Alpine hut prices are generally rather higher, depending on location. Local tap water is safe and good; if drinking wine ask for 'tap water' or 'normal water' along with it. The local mini-supermarkets supply bread, cheese, ham, salami, milk, coffee, cereals etc., but take tea bags! Tubs of 'Rama' margarine are more practical for the visitor than butter.

3. LOCAL TRANSPORT

(1) Buses

Slovenian buses are large, air conditioned and comfortable. They run as often 5-10 minutes before time as 5-10 minutes after. There is normally a board on the windscreen with 'where from' on the left and 'where to' on the right. A ride up the 24 hairpin bends to Vršič, looking across to the pillars of Prisojnik, is a memorable experience and costs £2 in 2006.

The bus service operating on the east-west road from Rateče to Ljubljana via the bus station at Kranjska Gora runs every hour for most of the day.

There are at time of writing 6 buses a day over Vršič during July and August only. (However, these two months provide the best opportunity for snow-free scrambling in any case (see below).)

There are two bus companies operating separate time tables. Be sure to get both. In Kranjska Gora, the bus stops at the bus station and at a marked stop outside Hotel Lek at the southern end of the village.

The preference for car use among Slovenians and visitors from adjoining countries causes the summit of the pass to be cluttered, especially at weekends, and leaves the buses almost empty. It is a very useful service for visitors arriving by air and I hope it will be better patronised to avoid closure.

(2) Taxis

Taxis are listed in the Tourist Office booklet; I use Mitja Mertelj (see above). Prices for journeys to expedition starting points at Vrata, Vršič and Tamar are reasonable: especially for a full car or mini-bus load.

(3) Cycle hire

Cycle hire is available in the village at reasonable prices and a cycleway along the old railway track parallel with the main road helps cycle access to the Planica and

Vrata valleys. Cycling up Vršič (800m of ascent) is for the very fit; a feat of endurance, which is tested in an annual cycle race.

(4) Car hire

This is expensive, particularly for a short return drive with a long expedition in between, and the restriction of having to return to the same point (unless using the car in combination with the bus). The car ride is included if you hire a local mountain guide.

(5) Lifts

It is my experience that lifts from Vrata and Vršič at least, are easy, but these roads become very quiet in the evenings! If further afield, at Trenta or Bohinj, it is as well to carry a passport in case the last bus is missed and overnight accommodation is needed.

4. LANGUAGE

To the ordinary English speaker, the Slovene language, spoken by about 94% of Slovenians, is almost impenetrable, but a smattering of knowledge of how it works helps avoid unnecessary confusion.

Like Gaelic or Latin, the words change form according to how they are used. Thus Triglav (ending 'ow' as in 'how'), but Triglavska severna stena (Triglav North Wall) and Triglavski dom na Kredarici (Triglav Hut on Kredarica), for which the starting point is Aljažev dom v Vratih ('j' always pronounced 'y') (The hut at Vrata named after Jakob Aljaž.)

Three Slovene expressions are needed:-
(a) 'Prosim' (like the Australian 'possum' with an 'r' included) meaning 'please'. (Always roll the 'r')
(b) 'Hvala' (like the Australian 'koala' substituting an 'h') meaning 'thank you'.
(c) 'Dober dan' meaning 'good day' - it is courteous to greet passers-by when out walking. ('Doberrr dan'!)

5. THE HUTS

The huts supply simple overnight accommodation with facilities, which vary from good basic to primitive. Take passport; no sleeping-bag is necessary. Drinks and meals may be bought at prices which are generally about 1½ times those in Kranjska Gora but varying according to the accessibility of the hut. An alternative to carrying sandwiches is to buy soup at a hut (halfway to a stew, with a hunk of bread). Unless a connoisseur, beware the Turkish coffee - an inch of strong bitter fluid, with half-an-inch of mud. Otherwise, coffee is good. Tea comes black and sweet with lemon.

(1) Mihov dom 1150m. Above bend number 4 on the road to Vršič. There are splendid views from the terrace, eastwards past the steep north end of Prisojnik. The bus may be picked up here after walking down from Vršič, to save the last 6km. to Kranjska Gora. It is a starting point for Špik and Kriška stena via Krnica.

(2) Koča na Gozdu 1226m. below bend number 10 on the road to Vršič. This is the starting point for the Hanzova pot on Prisojnik.

(3) Erjavčeva koča ("ErYAHsheva") 1525m. Above bend number 21 on the road to Vršič. This is a starting point for the Window Route on Prisojnik and close to the descent from Vršič by the old grassed road.

(4) Tičarjev dom 1620m. A few metres from the bus stop and car parking at the summit of the pass. This is a good point of call when returning from the routes above Vršič.

(5) Poštarska koča 1688m. 15 min. walk on the broad track over the hump from Vršič. There are splendid views from the terrace eastwards to the pillars of Prisojnik. This is a starting point, after refreshment, for the easy descent towards Kranjska Gora by the old grassed road.

(6) Koča pri izviru Soče (Soča Source Hut): 876m. In the deep Trenta Valley 1½ km. up a side road from the foot of the road down from Vršič (after bend number 48). This is a stopping point after the descent of Vršič on the south side, and a tourist trap - the river wells out of a cave in the crag above.

(7) Zavetišče pod Špičkom (Špička Hut) 2064m. This is high on the route from Vršič or from Trenta to the South Ridge of Jalovec. It is a small hut immediately below a rock cone visible from the Vršič-Trenta road.

(8) Dom v Tamarju (Tamar Hut) 1108m. This is situated near the head of the Planica Valley close to the Italian border, with restricted vehicular access from Rateče (see later). It is a starting point for the north side of Jalovec and a good point of call after descending from Vršič by Sleme.

(9) Koča v Krnici (Krnica Hut): 1113m. This is situated in the Krnica Valley, which runs south-east from the foot of the Vršič pass. Access is from Mihov dom (45 min.) or from Kranjska Gora (1½ - 2 hours). It is a stopping point on the way to Špik or Kriška stena, or a destination for a valley walk.

(10) Zasavska koča na Prehodavcih (Prehodavci Hut): 2071m. The hut is situated on the ridge at the top of a First World War mule path from Trenta and at the head of the Seven Lakes Valley down to Bohinj. It is a starting point for routes on Kanjavec and for the Špičje Ridge.

(11) Tržaška koča na Doliču (Dolič Hut) 2151m. Between Triglav and Kanjavec and accessible by a steep First World War mule path from Trenta. At or near the junction of 6 routes.

(12) Pogačnikov dom (Kriški podi Hut) 2050m. The hut is situated on the north-east skyline looking from Trenta, accessed by a steep First World War mule path. It is a good stopping point on the traverse from Krnica over Kriški podi and a focal point for other routes.

(13) Aljažev dom (Vrata Hut) 1015m. The hut is situated near the head of the Vrata Valley, with vehicular access from Mojstrana. It is a starting point for Škrlatica and for routes on the North Wall of Triglav.

(14) Triglavski dom (Kredarica Hut) 2515m. The is the highest hut on Triglav and a meteorological station, with access by routes from all directions and a starting/finishing point for the popular equipped East Ridge. It is large and comparatively well-appointed.

(15) Dom Valentina Staniča (Staničev Hut) 2332m. This is an alternative hut for Triglav from the east and a starting point for several peaks on that side.

Štanicev is an example of a more remote and basic hut. Supplies used to be brought in by pony, now by helicopter, and the water supply is rainwater collected in a tank. Sanitation is non-flush! But I found the cooking excellent, the service friendly (but no English) and the company cheerful.

6. SUMMER WEATHER IN THE JULIANS

It will be apparent that this is not the high Alps, clad In perpetual snow and ice. There is only a tiny glacier above the North Wall of Triglav, and a few permanent but variable snow/ice patches. But only in July and August are the high peaks clear of snow and ice, and even that cannot be fully guaranteed. In the Spring of 2001, there was late heavy snowfall, leaving ramps of hard snow persisting in late July in crucial places, such as the foot of the north face of Mala Mojstrovka, the ledge traverse eastwards from the summit of Prisojnik, and even low down, choking the gorge of Črna voda (Black Water) on the descent from Sleme to Tamar. In late August of the same year, I found the Prisojnik traverse completely clear, but had to avoid ramps of snow in hollows on the south side of the mountain, and I found that the traverse across the North Wall of Kanjavec was still closed. Then on 4 September came the first snow of the Autumn.

These conditions are the worst I have known in twenty years of summer visits and it may be a climatic aberration, although it is possible that late snow is a downside of global warming. Indeed, there was heavy Spring snow in 2006. It would therefore be advisable to take or arrange to borrow an ice axe, or at least, to have available one of the many route options which avoid the problem. Enquire in advance of a local guide, or ask on the way at one of the huts.

The more usual weather problem is thunderstorms. Sometimes there is a mere growling in the afternoon, sometimes a fearsome display of thunder and lightening with torrential rain, and ice forming on the summits. Then avoid or retreat from the highest places. A mini-folding umbrella is useful on lower walks for protecting head and shoulders as the rain usually comes straight down, but overtrousers are still required.

That said, I have known spells of ten days of brilliant weather, hot (but not humid) at Kranjska Gora, and pleasantly cooler at Vršič. In such conditions, the sudden heat is palpable when crossing bare south-facing rock.

7. THE DANGERS AND HOW TO MINIMISE THEM

The maps show as solid red lines 'marked alpine paths - easy'; as broken red lines 'marked alpine paths - rather difficult'; and as dotted red lines 'marked alpine paths - very difficult'. (In the Italian version 'via ferrata - difficilissima').

You can get into trouble losing even an easy path on lower ground, because of low-level crags, steep unstable slopes and ravines, to say nothing of the dense thickets found in the natural forests. To lose the path at higher levels is potentially lethal, as, in the area of this guide at least, they thread over and through vast crags of loose rock with no easy way down.

The marks comprise red rings with a white centre painted on the rock, and short red lines indicating direction - vertical, horizontal or forming an angle at turns in the route. There can be problems in following the marks in some places, e.g. on leaving a forest clearing or when the path leaves an open area for dwarf pine thickets, or in areas of scree, where there are no static rocks to mark. Sometimes the route suddenly leaves an obvious terrace for a steep rock groove up or down. If in doubt, go back to the last mark and try again. Similarly, if on slabby rock the scrambling becomes more difficult, you will be off-route: at awkward points on marked routes, there are fixed pegs or wire cables.

The complexities of the ground are often such that it does not necessarily help to see the destination or the general lie of the land. I have crossed the Kriški podi plateau, which consists of chasms and crags, several times in mist following the marks, but twice in clear weather had to retrieve the route by going round cave shafts and crossing fissures in sight of the Pogačnikov Hut.

The dangers of hard snow and ice, localised in time and space, have already been noted. Beware also that limestone becomes very slippery when damp or wet - but it also dries very quickly after rain, and seepages are not usually extensive.

I consider that the chief danger of taking a fall is in descending easier slabby rocks partly overlain with loose stones - take small steps and mind where you put your feet!. If the rock is awkward in descent or if it is steep, or holds are sloping, face inwards and look between your feet. Do not lose concentration until terra firma is truly reached. I know from experience that even a small tumble among stones can deliver heavy punishment - unlike the turf of most of our own hills.

Lastly, there is the cause of most Slovenian mountain fatalities, namely falling stones. The rock ledges are often laden with stones ready to be released by human feet or even by a chamois or ibex (and on rock climbs by the movement of a climbing rope). I have been hit three times and I can say that stones do not fall like autumn leaves: they strike like bullets.

Therefore, you should always wear a climbing helmet in steep places. Never mind the local youth who often do not: they are the despair of the mountain rescue and medical services. You may still be struck on another part of the body and even knocked off, so flatten against the rock and clip on to a peg or cable if possible, if you hear falling stones. Avoid looking up. Beware of people above, particularly in gullies. If in a party, keep close together and do not cross on loose stones above your friends! The crags are often deserted, but there is still the odd stone-fall: the late snow slopes below the unfrequented parts of the Mala Mojstrovka crag will be found littered with rock fragments.

On any but the shortest of mountain excursions, you should as a matter of course, carry torch and whistle, and, without overloading, some food, drink and spare clothes.

8. TECHNIQUES FOR 'EQUIPPED' ROUTES (VIA FERRATA)

The aim is self-protection or self-belaying. A climbing harness is recommended, although I dispense with the leg loops and just use the broad webbing belt with loop attachment. Fix to this by means of a screwgate karabiner two stitched webbing 'slings' (loops) with a twist-lock quick-release karabiner (I use 'DMM Wales') on the end of each. The lengths of the slings should allow the karabiner to be clipped to the fixed pegs or cable at about finger tip distance from your body: the sling should not sag to your knees, but you must be able to reach out with it. The idea of course is to facilitate continuous security, e.g. by clipping on to a cable beyond its holding peg before releasing the karabiner already clipped. You may not need to use both karabiners when the footing is good - e.g. when walking along ledges (unless overhung). Petzl do a 'Zyper' with a figure-of-8 device at point of attachment to the harness for shock absorption; and such a device is strongly recommended in case of a fall when clipped on to a steep or vertical cable high above a peg.

Telescope down and put away walking poles in good time when hands are needed. (I was once 'assaulted' by a Slovenian woman who did it for me as she thought I was heading into danger - but don't go in hope!) Always clip on before taking photos. Carry your camera in a padded wallet with a waist belt or other handy attachment.

9. MAPS REQUIRED

I use 3 maps:-

(1) 'Triglav' Scale 1:25000 covering the whole Triglav massif from just south of Kranjska Gora southwards to Bohinj;

(2) 'Kranjska gora' Scale 1:25000 covering the area from the Austrian border southwards past Vršič.

(3) 'Trenta' Scale 1:25000 which is necessary for the west side of the Trenta area and the southern approaches to Jalovec.

All are available locally or from Edward Stanford Ltd., 12-14 Long Acre, London WC2E 9LP.
www.stanfords.co.uk

The sketch maps in this guidebook are indicative only, or for supplementary guidance, and must not be regarded as a substitute for the published maps, which are indispensable for walking and scrambling in their respective areas.

10. LOCAL GUIDES

The harder routes described here may all be enjoyed by any serious walker with experience in scrambling e.g. of the Crib Goch ridge on Snowdon, Sharp Edge on Blencathra, the Aonach Eagach ridge in Glencoe, An Teallach in Wester Ross. But if in doubt, employ a local guide, at least initially.

The Tourist Office Kranjska Gora information booklet (already mentioned) lists mountain leaders and alpine guides.

The 'List of Mountain Guides & Guiding Tariffs' covers all registered members of the Slovenian Mountain Guides Association, and is available from:-
   Združenje gorskih vodnikov Slovenije (ZGVS)
   Dvoržakova 9
   1000 Ljubljana
   SLOVENIA

(Tel: 00386 4137 8137   Fax: 00386 1432 2140)
(e-mail: info@zdruzenje-gvs.si)
(website: http://zdruzenje-gvs.si)

The maps show that most of the rugged mountains in this area have no marked paths whatsoever. Such are the difficulties, complexities and dangers of the terrain, that I strongly recommend the employment of a local registered guide if you want to explore these mountains away from the marked paths.

I also recommend a registered guide for rock climbing: even on the easier climbs, route-finding is normally very tricky, and much of the rock is loose.

11. ESTIMATES OF TIME AND EFFORT

Distances are difficult to measure because of the twists and zig-zags of the routes. Height gained is useful, particularly for estimating effort, but does not allow for the time required to move safely on steep or chaotic rocks. Moreover, it may take as long to go down as up.

I have quoted the heights in metres, and the standard time stated on Slovenian maps, signs etc. I find them fairly consistent, with a few exceptions. Descending to Trenta from the Pogačnikov Hut and having passed a sign saying 'Trenta 4 hours' it was disconcerting to pass another saying 'Trenta 5 hours'. In the event we pushed down in 3½ hours with time for a drink before the bus back to Kranjska Gora.

Strong walkers may knock one-third off standard times. You can calibrate your performance or that of your party, and use it to assess the possibilities for longer one-day expeditions.

It is of course possible to stay overnight in the high-level huts, thereby avoiding pressures of time, and the effort of additional initial ascents. This would be necessary for longer tours, and may be particularly enjoyable in periods of settled weather, but I have concentrated on day excursions.

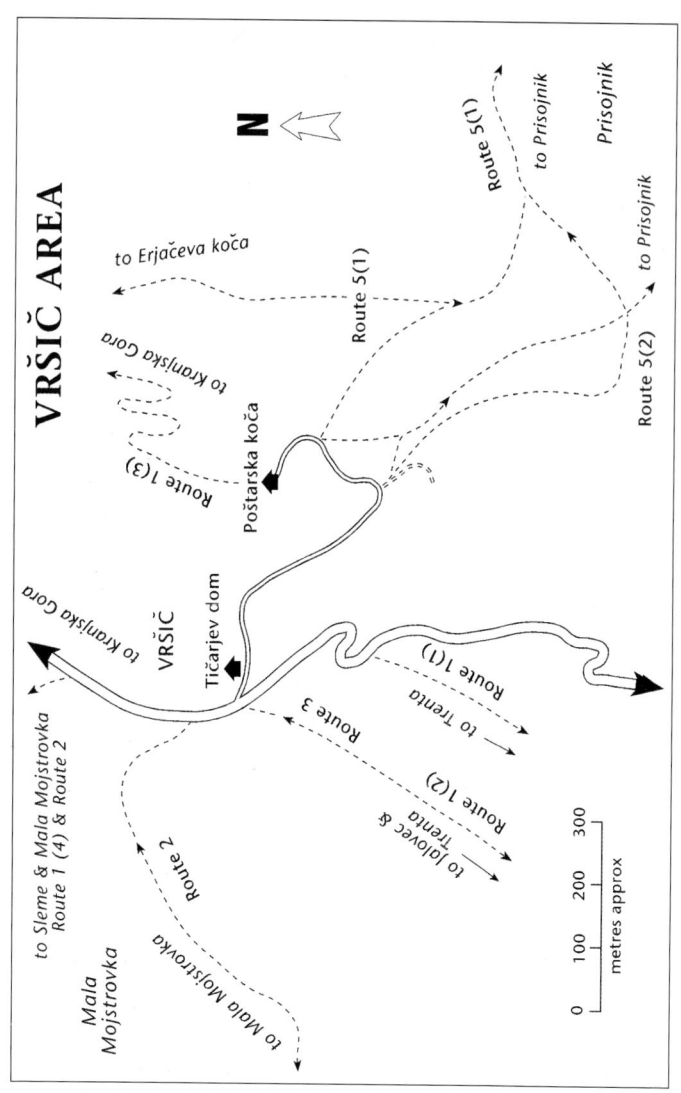

THE ROUTES

1: MAINLY DOWNHILL FROM VRŠIČ

These are all easy walks on mainly good paths, virtually danger-free and needing no special equipment. On good days, the times stated should be extended to allow for leisurely stops.

(1) TO TRENTA

(Sketch maps: Vršič Area; West of Vršič)
Time: 1½ hours

From the summit of the pass, walk down the main road towards Trenta, past bends numbers 25 and 26 followed by a terraced section, then down right at a brass plaque (on shaky posts - how long will it last?) indicating 'Trenta 1H'. (The path must have been in better condition then.) The route is at present only intermittently marked and not altogether clear in the upper sections. In particular, about 100m. past a large waymarked boulder, turn off the broad track down to the right on an initially rough path; and after another section of broad track, about 120m. down a steep cobbly section, turn left down a steep narrow rutted bouldery path, which emerges eventually on to another broad and easy track. Turn down this track.

This continues gently into a series of well-engineered zig-zags mostly carpeted with beech leaves, past a rock face inscribed as a memorial to Austrian army sappers in 1915. Then the path drops more steeply to emerge amongst large boulders on a balcony with views over the Zadnja (Inner) Trenta Valley. A good place to stop!

The engineered path continues down steeply in tight corkscrews to join a noisy stream, which is eventually crossed by a new plank bridge. Then a short almost level section near the bottom of the valley through a spruce wood and past a summer cottage (No.70 Trenta) and left down a passage between old stone walls to the tarred road a few metres east of the Soča Source Hut. From the hut go back down the road, and continue for about 1½ km. to the bus stop at the main road junction at the foot of the pass.

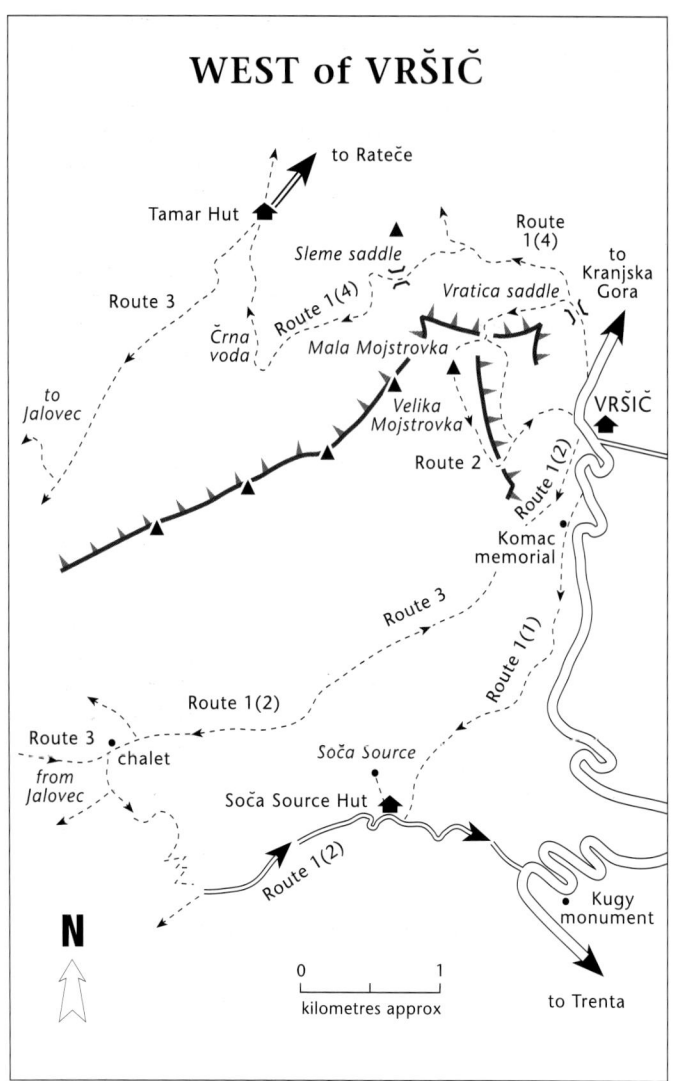

Notes

(1) Beside the path, not far from the start, stands a memorial shrine to Andrei Komac who died here on 10 December 1908. He was local guide to Julius Kugy, the greatest explorer of the Julian Alps, whose statue stands a little way up the hill from the road junction at the end of the walk.

In 'Alpine Pilgrimage' (1934) Kugy says "...among the Trenta poachers, Andreas was the boldest of the bold". He hunted chamois, hence his knowledge of the crags. I have been told that there was desperate poverty in Trenta when the minerals, which were mined there, ran out. Kugy, an Austrian living in Trieste, would summon his guides by telegram to help him on his ascents.

Later developments did not please him: "After those Friends of the Mountains [the makers of the equipped routes], with paint pot, spade, pitons and cables, comes a howling mob, clamouring for provisioned huts, high inns, or in fact, Alpine hotels. They think and dream of beer." Join the club!

(2) The Soča Source Hut is a tourist honey-pot, being readily accessible by vehicle, and the starting point for visiting the river source, which is a famous tourist spectacle. Yet the hut location remains pleasant, with tables outside above the rushing stream, and with steep wooded mountains all round.

The source is reached in 10-15 minutes by a steep rocky eroded path. At forks, take the right-hand option (the other paths go into the stream bed below the source). Finally, the path levels, and a traverse across a steep rock face with foot holds and a cable handrail leads to the final steps down on to boulders and a cave mouth, where the water wells up or gushes out according to conditions. There is a recess halfway along the traverse, which serves as a passing place.

(2) TO TRENTA VIA THE TRAVERSE

(Sketch maps: Vršič Area; West of Vršič)
Time: 3 hours (to road end)

By the kiosk on the west side of the road at the summit of Vršič is a rocky platform/viewpoint. Walk over this to find painted signs for Špička and Jalovec. The path is clear but rough at the start, after which it is excellent underfoot, virtually all the way. From Vršič it drops down below a crag and rises in steps over a tree-clad rocky spur with two short sections of cable (no special equipment needed), then with lesser undulations crosses steep open grassy slopes and woodland, mainly larch, with magnificent views over Trenta, dominated by Bavški Grintavec (2347m.) Some sections are a little airy, but the path shelf is adequately wide. Then the side slope lessens, the woodland, now mainly spruce and beech, becomes continuous and a small private chalet comes into view.

Immediately past the chalet, turn down left. The path is rather but not excessively steep and is pleasant underfoot. Take care not to lose it, because it develops into a series of wide engineered zig-zags down craggy slopes. These slopes are under beech woods and clear of undergrowth so there is a possibility of a trundling stone being released.

Suddenly, the valley bottom is reached: the path levels on the edge of a flat meadow with a chalet nearby and arrives at a picnic area close to the vehicular road end.

Turn left down this road and walk for 1½km. to the Soča Source Hut. This is a further 1½km. from the bus stop on the main road.

See Note (2) above on the hut and the river source.

(3) TO KRANJSKA GORA

(Sketch maps: Vršič Area; Prisojnik Area)
Time: 4hours

From the summit of Vršič, walk up the broad track past the Tičarev Hut, then left at the main junction and swing back on to the north side of the knolly ridge, which crosses the top of the pass, and arrive at the Poštarska Hut at 1688m. elevation. This is a splendid place to stop, with views from the terrace over the top of the forest down towards Kranjska Gora, and across to the many-pillared north-west face of Prisojnik. Immediately below the terrace is a broad grassed-over road, the former road over the pass. (The Poštarska Hut was the post house.) Walk a few metres back down the track from the hut and join the old road which trends down leftwards across the slope, looping back to the right in a wide elbow after 6-7 minutes. Continue down that road in increasingly big hairpins, at first among scattered trees and bushes - a good place to linger on a hot day - and gradually into beech and spruce forest.

The Erjačeva Hut comes into sight not far from a north-west hairpin and the walk may be cut short there, by cutting across a steep bank on a narrow marked path to the hut, then picking up a bus on the main road at a marked stop about 150m. below the entrance road to the hut. But continuing the long gentle zig-zags, you eventually join the main road past a private chalet standing in woodland.

Now walk uphill on the main road for about 300m. to find a path (poorly marked at present) leading downhill beside a torrent bed. (After heavy rain, it is itself a torrent bed!) The path, badly eroded in places but with signs of ancient construction, leads down over streams crossed by foot bridges and gradually improves until after about 1km. it emerges on to the main road. Follow the road downhill round the bends or take the steep short cuts, to the Mihov dom above bend number 4 - a good place to take a break or wait for the bus.

If walking on to Kranjska Gora, go a few metres down the road to a steep rough path dropping down to a broad track. Follow this to a junction and turn right down a roughly surfaced road to a car parking area. Pass through this area and, approaching a ford across a river, turn left and cross a plank bridge. Walk past a private chalet and over a meadow. Pass a memorial shrine on the left, then turn left down a track beside the main torrent bed away from Krnica and continue along the track crossing the torrent bed and following down the river to join the main road beside a new bridge. Then walk past Jasna lake and restaurant, past Hotel Lek and into Kranjska Gora.

(4) TO TAMAR AND RATEČE VIA THE SLEME SADDLE

(Sketch maps: Vršič Area; West of Vršič; Guidebook Area for whole route.)
Time: 5 hours to Rateče

The whole walk is easy but lengthy, with a 700m. descent from the Sleme saddle to Tamar, then about 7km down the Planica valley to Rateče or about 11km. if continuing through the meadows and along the old railway to Kranjska Gora. It is still a splendid walk, retaining the most spectacular elements, if cut short by returning to Vršič from Sleme.

From the summit of Vršič walk back along the main road north until the road begins to dip down; there a plaque indicates the start of the route to Sleme and Tamar. The path is clear and well-marked, but rough in places. It rises through pine bushes and across scree slopes on a generally well-graded ascent to the Vratica saddle at 1799m. There are good views back towards Prisojnik, then at Vratica the magnificent north wall of Mala Mojstrovka bursts into view. (To see it from Kranjska Gora you have to go to the furthest away end of the village near the bus station, because of intervening high ground.) From Vratica, a scree path turns off left for Mala Mojstrovka, but follow the main path dipping and winding through a beautiful zone of scattered larches, pine bushes and other shrubs, with large jagged rocks and scree. This is the natural tree-line zone that is almost absent from Britain. Passing the turning for a steep and rough descent via the Grlo saddle, continue along the main path rising a little past a plaque to fallen climbers, set in a rock face, to arrive at a sharp larch-clad saddle at 1500 metres elevation abutting a huge rock wall. There, on a fine day a second surprise view appears: Jalovec! - from this angle a singularly beautiful mountain with its roofed summit and supporting pinnacles.

A diversion may be made here by ascending the gently sloping pastures on the right to the summit of Sleme itself, which is from other aspects, a sharp rock peak. It provides a good viewpoint.

From the saddle begins the long descent to Tamar, so if considering returning to Vršič, the saddle is the place to make the choice. If continuing, a clear path descends steep grassy slopes amongst larch trees, then more gently down a stony area into beech woods, trending leftwards and steepening towards the top of a stony ramp. Care is needed on this ramp as the way is steep and badly eroded. It turns into the bottom of the ravine of the Črna voda (Black Water), following the foot of the right-hand wall on scree and boulders. (In July 2001 the ravine was still choked in deep hard snow.) There is a danger here of stones trundling over the edge from the gentler slopes above. The path suddenly emerges on to an open stony slope which levels off to form the floor of a wide forested valley. Then through the trees the Tamar Hut is seen. It stands at 1108 metres elevation looking out over a beautiful open pasture below a horseshoe of crags dominated by Jalovec.

The floor of the Planica valley beyond the open pasture is filled with beech forest. The map shows a footpath and a vehicular track. Be sure to find the start of the footpath, which is pleasant underfoot. The path rejoins the track after 3km., following which is a barrier and a sign declaring that, with the aim of "reducing the harmful effects of motorised traffic on the environment" the road is permanently closed to motor vehicles from 1 November to 30 April, and from 1 May to 31 October from 8am to 6pm. Continue along the road past the ski jumps and over the main road to Ratece, 4km. from the barrier. The bus terminus is a few metres left from the T-junction in the village.

Alternatively, turn right past the Planica Hut on a winding route through meadows to the old railway track running eastwards to Kranjska Gora (8km.). The old railway has been well tarred over to provide a fast route for cycles, roller blades, trainer skis etc., which may pass silently at speed!

Note

(1) 'Tamar' means 'enclosure' - the original building at Tamar was a shepherd's cabin within an enclosure for sheep and goats. Cheese was last produced here in 1925, and the people of Ratece still have grazing rights in the valley.

(2) **Vitranc** (1576m.) and **Ciprnik** (1764m.) These two summits stand at either end of an isolated steep-sided densely wooded ridge close above Kranjska Gora. Vitranc looks down on the village over ski slopes, and there is a tourist chairlift to the top, which I have never used. The broad undulating ridge to Ciprnik, 2km. away, has a marked path. The summit of Ciprnik rises above the woods in a steep rocky knob, and provides spectacular views on a clear day.

There is an unmarked path up Vitranc from the top of the ski slopes which winds up steeply under the chairlift. When leaving it at the top, be sure to note the way back to it under the trees, as all the slopes are very steep and loose. There are other unmarked paths: they require great care to follow as they are apt to disappear under stones and beech leaves, and in places it may be wise to leave your own temporary markers to ensure safe return.

2. MALA MOJSTROVKA: THE TRAVERSE FROM THE NORTH

(Sketch maps: Vršič Area; West of Vršič)

Elevation 2332m.; 721m. of ascent from Vršič.
Time: 2½ hours ascent; 1½ hours descent.

The ascent of the North Wall provides an excellent introduction into serious equipped routes (via ferrata), being steep and exposed but well secured except for a short slabby section near the start. This steep ascent is the Hanzova pot (pot = marked trail), named after the guide who first fixed the equipment in 1928. (Distinguish this route from the Hanzova pot of Prisojnik, Route 5(3) of this book, which is longer and more difficult.)

It is used as a descent for three classic rock climbs on Mala Mojstrovka, namely the Kaminska smer (Chimney Route) which splits the crag, the adjoining Severni raz (North Ridge), and the Deržajeva smer which uses the gully over to the left and its containing ridge. As a training exercise the descent of the Hanzova pot (following the ascent) is to be recommended for the experience, because in contrast to British crags, climbing down is unavoidable on major routes in the Julians.

From the summit of Vršič walk back along the main road north until the road begins to dip down; there a plaque indicates the start of the route to Sleme and Tamar. Follow this path (see Route 1(4)) to the Vratica saddle at 1799m. Then turn left up the scree path, ascending and descending a little and traversing across scree to a final steep scree ascent to the plaque at the foot of the rock.

Having donned helmet and harness in a place safe from stonefall, start with the pegs up the beginning of a massive overhung ramp, most of which is unequipped. There are large rock holds but care is needed where loose stones are lying, particularly if descending the same way. After the ramp there are pegs and cables for security all the way up the crag. An airy traverse on pegs is followed by a ladder-like section, then ledge traverses with cables for security. After about 300m. of ascent, the angle eases, the equipment ceases and the route becomes an easy scramble up blocky rocks to the summit.

Page i

1. Razor (left) and Prisojnik from Hotel Lek

2. Kranjska Gora – village centre

3. Looking south over Kranjska Gora to Prisjonik

Page ii

4. Above Trenta (Route 1(2))

5. Tourists near Soča Source

6. Old road from Vršič

7. Prisjonik from Postarška Hut (Devil's Pillar centre right)

8. Mala Mojstrovka from Vratica saddle

9. The Sleme saddle   *10. In the Črna voda ravine*

11. Tamar Hut and Jalovec

12. The path from Tamar

13. Vratica from Route 2

14. Ascent of Mala Mojstrovka
(Climber: Barrie Brown)

15. Summit of Mala Mojstrovka
from top of crag (Route 2)

16. Stone chute, Mala Mojstrovka

17. Špička Hut on Jalovec

18. Jalovec from southeast

19. Jalovec – South Ridge

20. Path down towards Špička Hut

21. *Prehodavci Hut   (Vršac on left, Kanjavec on right)*

22. *Špičje Ridge from near Triglav Lakes Hut*

23. *The Prehodavci - Dolic Traverse*

24. *Prisojnik: start of equipped sections of Route 5 (1)*

25. *The first steep section of Route 5 (1)*

26. *The Maiden's Face from Route 5 (1)*

27. The crux of the ascent

28. The bulge on the crux

29. The Great Window of Prisojnik from the road

30. Approaching the Window

31. Climbing the Window

32. Through the Window

33. Summit of Prisojnik from the west

34. Razor and Triglav from the summit of Prisojnik

35. Approaching the East Window (Route 5 (1))

36. Škrlatica group and Špik from Gozd Martuljek

37. Ascending Kriška stena

38. On Kriška stena in mist

39. Pogačnikov Hut from Bovška vratica

40. *Partizan Memorial and Triglav*

41. *Cmir from Triglav*

42. *Mali Triglav and Kredarica Hut from summit of Triglav*

43. *Tominškova (Route 8(3)) looking back to saddle*

Page xii

44. On Tominškova

45. On Tominškova

46. To the summit ridge of of Rjavina (Route 8(4))

47. The step on the ridge (Climber: Dušan Polajnar)

48. The Prag (Route 8(2))

49. Triglav from Rjavina

From the summit of Mala Mojstrovka, Velika Mojstrovka may be visited by a scree walk and a short rise up jagged rocks, and it is possible to continue further along the ridge, with magnificent views of Jalovec; but unless rock-climbing, you must return the same way.

The descent from the summit of Mala Mojstrovka to about 1800m. elevation is by a tedious route of scree on slabby rock: it is best to follow as nearly as possible the crest of the ridge, then, at a sharp notch, turn left through the notch and either run the scree down to Vršič or take the path traversing to the left and turning down through pine bushes. The scree is worn to bedrock in the uppermost section, which I consider dangerous, and in any case I believe the practice of scree-running to be environmentally unfriendly. It provides entertainment for trippers sitting outside the Tičarjev Hut at Vršič.

If you are content to descend from the top of the equipped route without going on to the summit, there is another way which is unmarked and requires clear weather. After the end of the fixed equipment, the marked route continues up left to the crest of a spur. From the crest, instead of continuing to the summit, head down the scree towards Vršič and swing right to a descending traverse below crags, which joins the main descent route below the notch. This alternative route is much easier than the descent from the summit.

Of course, Mala Mojstrovka may be climbed as a walk up and down the descent route – as a penance! Or better, if you need to avoid the North Wall and are confident of the route-finding, reverse the unmarked descent route described above; then pick up the marks ascending to the summit, so as to include the easy blocky scrambling, with fine views.

3. JALOVEC:
THE TRAVERSE FROM TAMAR TO VRŠIČ

(Sketch map: West of Vršič for start and finish; Guidebook Area for whole route.)

Elevation 2643m.; 1537m. of ascent from Tamar.
Time: 5-6 hours ascent; 5 hours descent to Vršič.

The route follows the spectacularly jagged skyline of the North-West Ridge or close to it. I found it very soundly 'equipped' on the rock sections; just a long way up to get there, and a long way to Vršič. Unfortunately, I did not take detailed notes, and the weather was misty.

Start by taking a taxi to Tamar (before 8am - note the restrictions on motor vehicles mentioned at the end of Route 1(4)). Immediately behind the hut, pick up the signs for Jalovec and follow the path up the valley floor, which is almost flat at first then with an increasing slope, for about 3km. from the hut.

Here turn steeply up to the right out of the valley floor on a rough marked path. Continue across slopes of mixed stones and grass rising to the Kotovo Saddle at 2138m. Turn left up the arête and follow this easily to the foot of the steep rock. Here, put on via ferrata gear for the rock ascent. The route goes to right and to left of the crest, then up a big chimney bristling with spikes, back to the crest. Finally, the route drops down on the right-hand side, crosses a double gap, well secured, and ascends the final peak of Jalovec by traversing to the right, then by open scrambling to the top.

From the summit, follow the broad, well-marked South Ridge among large blocks, then turn abruptly left off the ridge down the face by grooves and ledges to a stony terrace. Turn right, ascending a little, then follow a descending traverse of the face of Veliki Ozebnik. Towards the end, there are pleasant ramped ledge paths with cable handrail and plentiful wild flowers. Descend steeply and cross a stony bowl and up to the Špička Hut below its distinctive pinnacle. All difficulties are now past. A short cut is possible, missing out the hut, but a visit is recommended.

From the hut, descend through stony ground and dwarf pine to enter the woods above the private chalet mentioned in Route 1(2) and thence take the undulating traverse to Vršič.

Variant

About 1km after Špička, a path down to Trenta may be taken as an alternative, but the distance to the main road is not much less.

OTHER ROUTES

1. A straightforward and more easily arranged expedition is to Jalovec and back from Vršič. This reduces the ascent to about 1,100m. (allowing for undulations) with a total distance of about 20 kilometres. Going faster than age now permits, I have done the trip there and back in 9 hours.

(2) A round trip from Tamar (permitting the use of a cycle from Kranjska Gora) may be achieved, and has been recommended to me, but I have not yet done it. Continue up the valley floor from the hut past the turn for the route described, then at the start of the great couloir, climb steeply to the left up Jalovška Škrbina, then work round past Golicia and up to the stony terrace mentioned above in the descent from the South Ridge of Jalovec. Thence ascend to the summit of Jalovec, and return to Tamar by the North-West Ridge.

3. From a little beyond the Tamar Hut there is a route rising steeply north-westward to Srednja Ponca (1120m. of ascent, 3-4 hours), Zadnja Ponca and Visoka Ponca, all on the north-south ridge forming the Italian border. I have not climbed this route.

Note: On 27 December 1900, Julius Kugy and four others, all on one rope, made the first winter ascent of Jalovec. They ascended the great couloir from Tamar and the slabby face above the terrace to the south ridge described above in descent. During the return down the face, the middle man fell, followed by Kugy as a slab of ice gave way, but above him his guide Joze Komac, "a Trentana, and one of the most desperate poachers I have ever known" "was standing in crampons on dry rock and had anchored himself with all his strength", thereby saving the party from disaster.
(Julius Kugy, 'Alpine Pilgrimage' 1934).

4. SOUTH FROM TRENTA

(Sketch map: Trenta to Bohinj)

(1) BY THE SEVEN LAKES VALLEY TO BOHINJ

1471m. of ascent. 4 hours up, 5 hours down.

This is a long scenic walk of no difficulty but great character.

Take the early bus over Vršič to the far end of the village of Trenta, over the bridge. Walk about 600m. further along the road, and turn left up a rough vehicular track at a sign for Prehodavci. The elevation here is about 600m.

The track winds uphill, then drops a little over a bridge and continues to the right. A hundred metres or so after the bridge, turn off uphill to the left on a marked route which becomes an engineered mule path (constructed in the 1914/18 war). It passes above a modernised chalet and winds on uphill through woodland.

Avoid short cuts, marked or unmarked. A torrent bed is crossed by a new log bridge. This is followed by a level section, then zig-zags up an increasingly craggy slope where the path is cut out of bedrock in places. The path gradually swings left and becomes a balcony overlooking a ravine on the right, which peters out in a dry valley, where the path leaves the trees for pine bushes and open alpine pastures.

At the Čez dol saddle (1632m.), turn right and up steep zig-zags engineered through crags. The surface of the mule path becomes rough with loose cobbles. At the crest, the Prehodavci Hut comes into view on the left. It is perched on a ridge, with dramatic views over Trenta, and southwards over the Seven Lakes Valley, and is backed by the great crags of Vršac and Kanjavec to the east.

From the hut at 2071m. descend gradually over limestone pavement on a well-marked, well-used path partly on bedrock which is polished and slippery in places. The path passes the rock pool of Zeleno jezero, then the larger pool of Veliko jezero. On the left the peak of Velika Zelnarica rises sharply above scree slopes, followed by Mala Zelnarica, Kopica and Velika and Mala Tičarica in a continuous line. Away on the right, the slabby faces of Malo and Veliko Špičje form a high rim to the Seven Lakes Valley. (On the other side, they present a formidable craggy front above Trenta.)

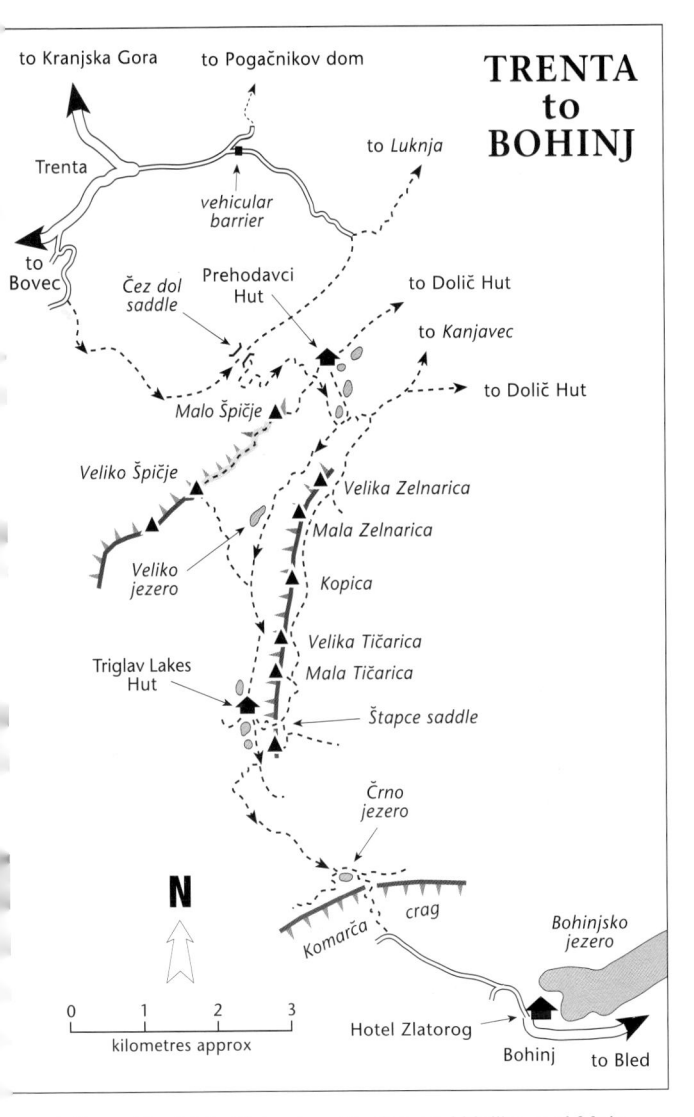

The Triglav Lakes Hut is reached immediately after a small reservoir, then after the hut the path crosses left before the Double Lake (Dvojno jezero) and rises over low knolls with open larch woodland. Then, after a sign

'Zlatorog Hotel 3.0 H' it drops steeply on firm but often polished rock into a heavily forested valley.

The path runs along this valley with little fall, close below steep crags on the left, which overhang the path in places. The dark rock-bound pool called Črno jezero (Black Lake) appears down on the right. The path continues round the far end of the lake (ignore a turn to the left), then on to the airy prow above the Komarča crags (at about 1400m. elevation) overlooking Bohinj.

The Komarča is descended by a series of ramps, with cable hand rail on the steepest sections. There is only one length of 3 or 4 metres in a gully where you have to step on rungs. Eventually, the gradients ease and the path becomes a zig-zag through sloping beech woods. I did not wear a helmet on this walk, but beware in case of stones bouncing down the steep open-floored beech wood. The path straightens as the slope eases and forms a T-junction into a broad track at about 650m. elevation, making the Komarča descent some 750m. Turn left. The track descends gradually and becomes a road past renovated chalets in the flat area at the head of Bohinj Lake (Bohinjsko jezero) then over a bridge to the bus terminus at the rear of the Hotel Zlatorog.

With luck you can catch a Ljubljana-bound bus and change at Lesce for a Rateče bus to Kranjska Gora; but changes at Bled, Lesce and Jesenice are all possible - prior research at the Tourist Office is advised.

(2) VARIANTS

(i) Alternative route from Trenta to Prehodavci

Leave the main road at the bus stop on the hairpin bend at the north end of the village, and walk along the gravelly vehicular track, almost level at first, then gradually rising. At 1½ km., pass the permitted road end and vehicular parking at the junction with the path to Pogačnikov dom. Pass through fields and by chalets into the forest, the trail rising more sharply, and emerge into an open area with views up the dramatically steep and narrow valley rising north-east to Luknja, and the more open valley rising south-west to the Čez dol saddle, with the vast rock wall of Kanjavec and its outlier Vršac on the left.

At the path junction is a finger post sign for Prehodavci. The path is clearly waymarked. It rises through pine scrub and up stony slopes. The surface is of loose small stones all the way, and the gradient is generally steep, so the ascent of about 700m. to the Čez dol saddle is tedious and demanding.

At the saddle, in larch trees, the path rises pleasantly in rock steps to join the engineered mule path already described. Although rough in this upper section, the mule path rises at an easier gradient and is a comparative relief.

This alternative route takes about the same time from Trenta as the route already described, which is much to be preferred. There is little saving for anyone arriving by car, because of National Park restrictions on the drive-in.

(ii) The Špičje Ridge

At a point about 1¼ km. short of the Lakes Hut on the route from Prehodavci to Bohinj, at some 1760m. altitude, a prominent sign indicates a route turning sharp right which ascends along a marked path to Veliko Špičje (2398m.) then along a fine but easy undulating ridge to Malo Špičje (2312m.) and down to the Prehodavci Hut.

(iii) The Tičarica - Zelnarica Ridge

From the north end of the Double Lake, a path rises eastward to ascend the line of crags near its south end by the Štapce saddle. (The upper section of this route is equipped.)

Thereafter, the path undulates disappointingly across slopes of scree and slab behind the crest of the dramatic crags seen from the main route, to reach a path crossing the stony wastes south of Kanjavec and providing an easy return to the Prehodavci Hut. At the south end of the ridge a short diversion leads to the summit of Mala Tičarica (2071m.) - a fine location.

(iv) Prehodavci to Dolič by Hribarice

By descending a little from the Prehodavci Hut into the head of the Seven Lakes Valley, it is possible to walk over Kanjavec (2568m.) to the Dolič Hut (Tržaška koča na Doliču) at 2151m. by an easy but stony route, or round the south side of Kanjavec over the Hribarice saddle (2358m.) through a stony wilderness.

From Dolič there is a spectacular First World War mule path cut out of steep crags down to the Zadnjica valley and Trenta. The surface and gradients are similar to the path between Prehodavci and the Čez dol saddle. The total descent to the main road is some 1500m.

There are paths from Dolič up to the South Ridge of Triglav or round the south side of Triglav to the Planika Hut or by a long descent to the Voje valley and Bohinj. For these routes, an overnight stop is indicated.

(v) Prehodavci to Dolič by the North Wall of Kanjavec

This route takes a spectacular line along scree ledges with little security by way of fixed equipment. I consider it easy but dangerous.

From the Prehodavci Hut, the route drops a little north-eastwards through deep turf and over smooth bedrock with painted waymarks, and passes above the uppermost pool of the Seven Lakes - an idyllic spot ringed by mountains - then climbs by rock steps and by zig-zags up steep scree to the sharp saddle between Kanjavec on the right and Vršac on the left.

The path then drops sharply by rock steps, ledges and steep scree down the Vršac side of the stony bowl between the uppermost crags of the North Walls of Vršac and Kanjavec. The way crosses this bowl on scree to become an almost level route across the North Wall of Kanjavec. It follows sloping scree ledges below a great bulging rock face for much of the way, disconcertingly changing ledges where the wall above is less steep. The fixed equipment comprises only a few short lengths of cable - the cable being unusually slack for Slovenia - and some pegs to hold where the rock bulges out over the ledge.

I was conscious that my helmet would have been of no avail against the angular 50 kg. blocks which appeared to have fallen recently.

Finally, the route rises round the receding crags and along wet overhung ledges into a bowl of block scree which is crossed to join the mule path about 15 minutes below the Dolič Hut.

I picked my way along this treacherous route with great caution, taking 3 hours instead of the prescribed 2, and missing the last bus to Kranjska Gora from Trenta after the long and magnificent descent down the mule path from Dolič (See above). In 2001, the route was closed all summer by hard snow.

NOTE

(1) The Zlatorog

The area of the walk to Bohinj is associated with the legend of the Zlatorog. He was a white, golden-horned chamois (but the statue at Jasna is more like an ibex!) who guarded a buried treasure. He was wounded by a hunter from Trenta, and where he dripped blood you will find cushions of the Triglav Rose. The Zlatorog recovered, and raged through the garden of the Seven Lakes Valley, laying it waste. (But I find it a delight!)

(2) The Seven Lakes (Triglav Lakes) Valley

The first botanical exploration of the valley was carried out by Balthasar Hacquet in 1777. Since then the valley has been famous for its rare and beautiful alpine flora. Some of the flowers may be seen growing in profusion near the path, some are scattered on scree and some are found in rock crevices. The area was declared an Alpine Protection Park in 1924 and formed the kernel of what was to be the present Triglav National Park. Tread lightly!

5. PRISOJNIK

The name 'Prisojnik' ('PrisOYnik') (2547m.) was for many years taken to be appropriate to this mountain, and has been extensively used on maps and in the literature. I now understand that the name **'PRISANK'** is not, as previously supposed, merely colloquial or imported from the German, but that it is the original and correct Slovene name. It is being increasingly adopted. On reprinting, I have retained 'Prisojnik' throughout this book, but readers should be aware of both names.

Prisojnik dominates the view south from Kranjska Gora with its long east-west ridge and short steep north ridge thrusting towards the village. At the east end is the subsidiary peak of Zadnji Prisojnik, with its needle's eye window clearly visible, and dramatic pinnacles continuing to the next mountain, Razor. At the west end is the dark recess containing the Great Window, before the mountain ends in the crags of Kraj sten, where it drops to the broad knolly ridge past which the motor road crosses at the pass of Vršič. The north ridge is steeply pillared on its west side. The south side of the mountain is mostly slabby rock, split up by short spurs.

Note: The 50m. high Great Window of Prisojnik (Veliko okno) is otherwise known as the Front Window (Prednje okno) and the East Window as Malo okno (Little, although huge) or Zadnje okno (Back or Inner).

The marked routes comprise:-

(1) a traverse up through the Great Window from the north, along the ridge (with a deviation on the south side) to the summit, and continuing eastwards mainly along ledges on the north side, through the East Window and down to the south;
(2) three routes on the south side;
(3) a route on the north-west face.

All routes on the south side start or finish on a path round the flank of the mountain. The routes will be described in turn.

(1) THE TRAVERSE THROUGH THE WINDOWS

(Sketch maps: Vršič Area; Prisojnik Area; see also 'Prisojnik Summit: south side - diagrammatic elevation')

To summit of Prisojnik, 4 hours, with 1,040m. of ascent; total return time for the traverse, 8-9 hours, with approx 1,170m. of ascent.

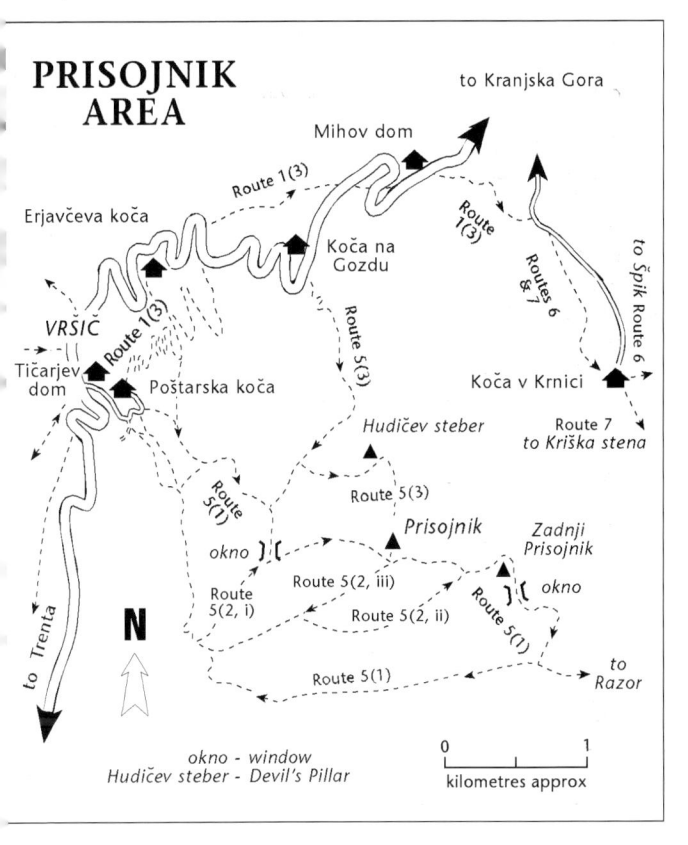

PRISOJNIK AREA

(sketch map showing routes around Prisojnik, with locations including Mihov dom, Erjavčeva koča, Koča na Gozdu, VRŠIČ, Tičarjev dom, Poštarska koča, Koča v Krnici, Hudičev steber, Prisojnik, Zadnji Prisojnik, okno, and directions to Kranjska Gora, Špik Route 6, Kriška stena, Razor, and Trenta)

okno - window
Hudičev steber - Devil's Pillar

0 — 1 kilometres approx

Start from the bus stop below the Erjavčeva Hut. Walk up the main road, over the car park and turn off to the right before the hut along a narrow path across steep banks, taking the upper route after crossing a washout below a concrete barrier. The narrow path gains an elbow of the old grassed road. Continue for a few metres on a steep rising path to cut the elbow and reach a gradually ascending section of the old road.

Follow the old road eastwards to the next elbow, then continue along the marked path through woodland, with some undulations, and cross a nasty steep washout. Finally cross to the rock wall over the foot of a scree slope which descends from the right hard against the side of a great crag.

Alternatively, start from Vršič as for Route (2)(lower), and when the broad saddle before the rock wall is reached, turn left at the sign for 'Okno Prisojnik' arrowed on the rock and descend about 100m. down steep scree. (The sign may be obliterated to discourage use.)

A second alternative, and probably the easiest and quickest way, starts at Vršič and continues up the rising track almost to the Poštarska Hut. At the top of the track, just short of the Hut, is a new (2006) signpost, indicating the way to the Window (okno). From there, a path descends to join the route from Erjavčeva to the same point.

Here is a plaque on an overhanging rock wall marking the start of the climb. Put on helmet and gear.

Traverse left with cables out on the cliff face, then up a near-vertical crack for about 30m. with cables and pegs, then diagonally left to land in dwarf pine bushes. Walk steeply up to a crest rising to right and follow this, continuing on scree and broken rock with occasional cables, until barred by a clean rock face. Do not turn left too soon!

Now follow a clear undulating traverse along grooves and ledges below a great red crag; turn a sharp corner and walk round a rock funnel to arrive at a 15m. crack straight up a bulging rock face, with rungs and cable on the right and then on the left. Land on an enclosed ledge and follow this into a little chimney. Climb the left wall on pegs to a cable round a block leading into a small cave, from which escape up left, inside the famous slit. This was once a squirm on polished rock, but has been made unsportingly easier by additional pegs further out.

Next climb some 25m. of steep rock with cables and large holds, then step through a cleft. Now make a winding ascent of scree paths and rock ribs and blocks, taking care to keep to the waymarks – there are false paths leading to dangerous places. So come eventually to a belvedere in full sight of the cathedral-like cavern lit by the Great Window. Take a short descent and traverse across a steep clean rock face, well secured, to the red scree forming the sloping floor of the cavern. Keeping initially well to the right on solid rock, walk up to a recess, then round into a groove and up an overhanging slab with cables and rungs. Emerge on the lip of the Great Window with views south over Trenta. Here you join an easier route which passes the Window, at a favourite point for watching climbers emerge from the depths and for looking through the jagged rock frame to the forest and winding road below.

The route then ascends rough slabs to the crest of the main ridge on excellent rock, then follows the broad crest. The summit of Prisojnik rises steeply ahead, but the route bears off right over scree and broken slabby rock (passing a sign and cable down right) before turning straight up for the last few metres. It used to be easy to lose the way crossing the rock ribs but in July/August 2001 the route was cleared of stones and freshly marked. It was still clear in 2006 – apparently volunteers work on it every Spring! (See Prisojnik Summit: south side - diagrammatic elevation')

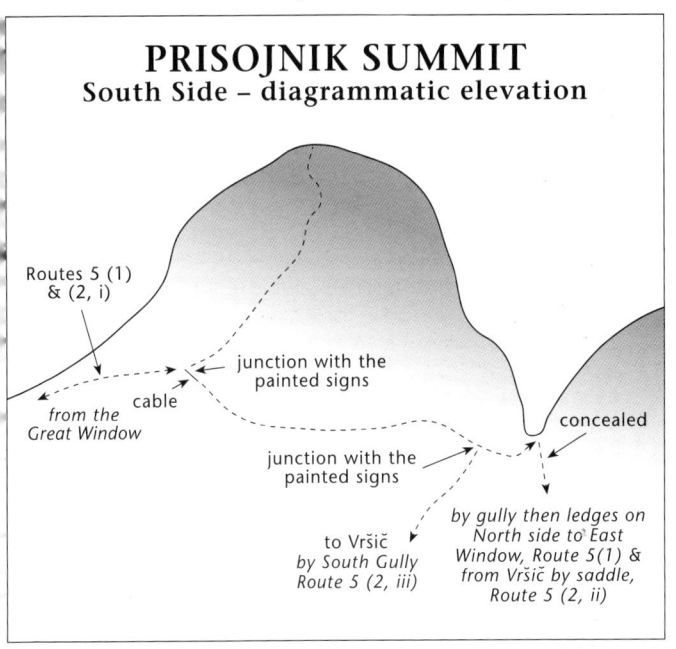

PRISOJNIK SUMMIT
South Side – diagrammatic elevation

Routes 5 (1) & (2, i)

from the Great Window

cable

junction with the painted signs

junction with the painted signs

concealed

to Vršič by South Gully Route 5 (2, iii)

by gully then ledges on North side to East Window, Route 5(1) & from Vršič by saddle, Route 5 (2, ii)

From the summit descend by the same way and traverse back until the sign and cable are reached. Turn sharp left down this cable to join a level path running east across slabs and scree, then descend a few metres to a sharp notch in the main spine of the mountain. (This part of the route follows roughly two sides of a triangle from the summit to avoid a band of steep loose rock - see again 'Prisojnik Summit: south side - diagrammatic elevation').

Step through the notch and descend a steep narrow gully on the north side of the mountain by pegs and cables for about 25m. then out to right as the gully becomes a chasm. Start a level scree path then turn down a cable for about 15m. followed by scree and slabby rock. Continue eastwards on a ledge path (partly cut out of rock) with fine views over Kranjska Gora and the Škrlatica range, then scramble up a sharp arête. Descend a crest, then slab and scree to a saddle in the main ridge, where you find a painted sign for Zadnje okno upwards, or down right for Vršič. (Described in ascent in Route (2)(ii))

Follow the marks upwards and round the subsidiary peak of Zadnji Prisojnik to reach a sustained ledge path on the north side. A chasm traverse and a sharp crest interrupt, but the ledge path resumes until, turning a corner, there suddenly appear the walls of the huge slot penetrated by the Zadnje okno. This window was greatly enlarged in the earthquake of 1997. The roof still looks unstable and there is a notice, warning (belatedly I think) of the dangers of rock fall. A hole under a gigantic fallen block takes you through to the south side.

There used to be a splendid 25m. descent of a chimney from the window, but, presumably because it might funnel stones, you must now move out to the left and down a very steep face. Take care - I thought some of the holds dubious in August 2000. Then follow a rock/scree path down to left (avoiding the couloir which debouches into a gigantic chimney), and round the foot of a clean crag past a rock nose, then down a 15m. slab followed by a zig-zag path down steep grass and slabs towards the brink of a crag.

Now take a rising rock traverse round a little gully before descending a scree path and a rock groove. Then about 50m. of excellent rough rock, and lastly a little chimney to arrive at a rubble couloir at the end of the crag. This is close under the great Škrbina pinnacle on the lowest part of the main ridge joining the next mountain.

Bear left down the rubble to gain a sloping mountain pasture with scattered rocks, and jewelled with flowers. (Once, sitting alone here, I found an ibex peering at me round a rock.) So down to join the main path returning to Vršič round the south side of Prisojnik. The path winds in slight undulations through dwarf pine followed by open larch woods, in and out of wide sandy gullies, then suddenly rises up a turf slope for about 200m. A few metres after the top of the re-ascent, Vršič with its welcome hut comes into distant view.

Note: The Maiden's Face

This feature forms part of the rock buttress on the left-hand side of the couloir below the scree or snow funnel under the Great Window. It is visible from upper parts of the road up Vršič from Kranjska Gora, from parts of the knolly area at the top of the pass, and from earlier sections of the route to the Great Window. The height from 'chin' to 'hairline' is about 35 metres.

In Slovene folklore, a girl giant, the 'Ajdi girl' lived among the rocks of Prisojnik above the pass. She was sweet-natured, and helped the porters who carried heavy loads between the valleys of the Sava and Trenta over the pass. She showed them the way in mist and snow.

One day the girl prophesied to a young mother that her small son would grow up as a hunter and that he would dare to hunt the Zlatorog - the chamois with the golden horns. Because of this terrible prophecy the Ajdi girl's sisters cursed her and turned her into stone. Today we can see her sad face looking down on us.

(2) THE SOUTH SIDE OF PRISOJNIK

(Sketch maps: Vršič Area; Prisojnik Area: see also 'Prisojnik Summit: south side - diagrammatic elevation')

(2)(i) To the summit past the Great Window

936m. of ascent; 3 hours 30 minutes.

There are two ways to begin the ascent: a lower and a higher route, both starting from Vršič.

To follow the lower route, walk up the broad track from Vršič past the Tičarjev Hut, then where the main track for Poštarska swings left, continue straight on, but almost immediately cut off from the track (part of the old road down to Trenta) up a narrow path through bushes and after 15m. bear right on an almost level path through pine bushes along the flank of the hill, Sovna glava, to a broad saddle. The path crosses three gully heads which (as at 2006) are tricky to negotiate.

To follow the higher route, continue uphill on the track towards Poštarska, and almost at the hut turn right at a sign (erected 2006) on to a path along the wide crest of the hill over low knolls, dropping eventually down a scree slope to the same broad saddle.

The lower route was 'closed' in 2006, but still very much in use; the route along the crest had eroded badly. I hope that the lower route will be 're-opened' (maybe with short lengths of cable across the gully heads), and the crest of the hill allowed to recover.

From the broad saddle bear right (south) on a good clear path forming a rising traverse across vast scree slopes, with the crags of Kraj sten high above on the left. The path continues closer below crags and through larch and dwarf pine, and winds up steeply to a crest, then levels out. (The continuation of this path round the mountain is the start or finish of Routes (2)(ii) and (2)(iii), and the finish of the Traverse, Route (1).)

Turn up left off the main path, steeply at first, partly on bedrock and through pine bushes, then more gradually up an open south-facing slope of alpine turf, and diagonally right to arrive on the sill of the Great Window at about 2300m. elevation.

From this point join route (1) (the Traverse through the Windows). Note that the start of next section - up past the Window to the ridge - is rather more demanding. It involves steep slabby rock but good natural holds, plus pegs at exposed points.

(2)(ii) To the summit by the saddle of Zadnji Prisojnik

950m. of ascent; 4 hours.

I consider that as far as the saddle, this route is easier and more interesting than the South Gully Route ((2)(iii)), which is the more usually recommended way. After the saddle however, it is, one might say, 'entertaining' comprising part of a ledge system and a steep gully on the north side pertaining to the Traverse Route (1).

Follow the preceding Route ((2)(i)) past Kraj sten and up to the crest, then instead of turning steeply upwards, continue on the main path. Pass the top of the re-ascent on the Traverse Route (signed for Razor). The path descends slightly then forms a rising traverse for about 600m. to the next junction, where a slab of rock bears a painted arrow pointing upwards with the word 'Prisojnik' (Route (2)(iii)), and another rock has a horizontal arrow indicating 'Zvoniki' (meaning 'Bell Towers' - the ridge pinnacles above the last part of thie climb). Follow the latter route, level at first then up a rising traverse across grassy slopes until a craggy pinnacle jutting out from the slope is approached. Now up and across a rock face on good steps with a handrail of cable, then a zig-zag path above a gully. Cross block scree (maybe a snow slope to cross or skirt) and diagonally right up the lower part of a rock wall, with good big holds but some loose rock. Now a steep rocky zig-zag easing into a grass slope, then round a nose below a rock spur. Now a rising traverse below crags to the next spur, steeply towards the end on loose stones, on round another grassy nose, then a gently rising path below crags becoming an exposed shelf with short lengths of cable round rock bulges. There follows a rising traverse up scree and slabs, then more steeply up shattered rock, with the route clearly marked, to a saddle on the spine of the mountain, with painted signs for 'Zadnje okno' (upwards), 'Prisojnik' (to left) and 'Vršič' (down right - the way you have come).

Turn left to join in reverse the Traverse Route for the section from the summit of Prisojnik to the saddle, and so reach the top.

(2)(iii) Descent by the South Gully

I find this route rather tedious and prefer all the foregoing for ascent, but it is commonly used in descent and is therefore described that way. It is a little tricky at several points.

Start the descent by following the section of the Traverse Route which continues from the summit to the notch where that route descends the steep gully on the north side. Here on the south side close to the notch, is a three-way painted sign. Turn down the steep twisting path on slabs and scree near the edge of the huge gully running down the south side of the mountain from the notch. Continue down on to a sloping rock nose. Keep on the nose until it drops steeply, then a wide shelf leads off to the right. Take this and continue diagonally down right into a bay of loose stones; then a scree terrace leads round the bay on to a nose. (The foregoing section of the route all the way from the summit was rendered much safer and easier to follow by clearance of loose stones on a defined route and painting of waymarks in July and August 2001 (and maintained since then by volunteers). Before that it was difficult to follow and potentially lethal, comprising indeterminate paths petering out in loose stones on slabby rock.

Descend the nose a little, then turn right down a short steep gully with a bed of red gravel, and a rising traverse to a line of rungs and pegs across a slab to a short blocky chimney down to the bed of a big gully. Follow down the foot of the left-hand wall and cross by the marks, then down the foot of the right-hand wall steeply on blocks of rock.

Now to another nose and down it, turning right just before a rock point with a cairn. Descend by pegs and two cables, and a slabby descending traverse into another gully with maybe a snow patch in the bed. Follow the base of the wall down block scree, steeply at the end to come out on another grassy nose, then a twisting eroded scree path.

Continue steeply down to the right, partly on bedrock, past a pinnacle to a steep loose zig-zag and across another stony bay, then ascend slightly on to a grassy slope and descend by a zig-zag and a traverse with short rock steps before the path eases and you arrive at the junction with the preceding Route ((2)(ii)).

(3) THE HANZOVA POT

(Sketch map: Prisojnik Area)

1400m. of ascent; 5 hours.

This splendid route is the only way up the north-west face of Prisojnik apart from hard and dangerous rock climbs. It had been allowed to fall into disrepair, but was re-equipped and re-opened in the summer of 1999. A local climber told me "They wanted to let it go, but the people revolted: they said 'It's our route'" The route constitutes a long rising traverse followed by a steep and complex ascent with some free scrambling.

Start at the Gozdu hut (1226m.) about halfway up to Vršič. Walk a few metres up the road, then drop down the marked route into a dry valley and up the other side, taking a zig-zag path up a cone of scree (clearly visible from the road) to arrive at the foot of the rock, and a plaque saying in several languages that the route is for experienced mountaineers only. The route rises across ribs and gullies with just one potentially dangerous section where it rises up a perched bank of loose earth and stones. There is a particularly deep gully before arriving at the foot of the Devil's Pillar (Hudičev steber), a 500m. Grade IV rock climb and a prominent feature of the face seen from the road.

Then suddenly, the marked route with tight cables descends and stops at a balcony overlooking a mini-glacier. In 1999 I found it a slope of steely rippled ice completely filling and blocking a couloir, but overcame it by climbing between a bulging block of rock and the side wall of the ice, then descending to the floor of a crevasse to reach the other side. In some conditions this mauvais pas may be just a soft snow plod, or it may be possible to crawl through the cave under the ice. Prior enquiry may be advisable!

There follows a section of walking and easy scrambling up a ramped traverse; then, signalled by another warning plaque, the upper part of the route turns straight up a rock wall (equipped) and above that enters a huge bowl of scree where the path, trending to the right hand side, is barely visible. It steepens, bearing leftwards into open slabs (which would be treacherous if wet), to arrive behind the top of the Devil's Pillar.

After that, the route follows a ledge rightwards across an overhanging cliff face, then straight up by free scrambling when the angle eases, and so on to a steep airy crest, arriving suddenly at the very summit of the mountain.

Variant

At the second warning plaque, instead of turning upwards at the rock face, continue the rising traverse to cross to the Traverse (Route (1)) below the Great Window.

6. ŠPIK: THE ASCENT FROM KRNICA

(Sketch maps: Prisojnik Area for start only; Guidebook Area for whole route.)

Elevation 2472m; approx. 1500m of ascent from Krnica. Time: 4 hours ascent; 3 hours descent to the valley.

This peak forms a symmetrical spire seen from the north, comprising the centre-piece of the dramatic backdrop to the meadows of Gozd Martulek. Here are 3 famous hard classic rock climbs, the Original (Dibona) Route (1924), the Direct Route (1926) and of course, the 'Direttissima' completed in 1978. However, the South Ridge is short and easy, requiring no specialised equipment, and best approached from Krnica.

The Krnica Hut, at 1113m., is a 1½ hours walk from Kranjska Gora, following the main road past Jasna Lake and continuing south at the new bridge, starting along the vehicular track and continuing after the meadow up the woodland path indicated below.

This approach can be reduced to 45min. by taking the bus to Mihov dom near the foot of Vršič. Return a few metres down the road, take a steep path descending to a broad track. Follow this to a junction and turn right down a roughly surfaced road to a car parking area. Pass through this area and, approaching a ford crossing a river, turn left and cross a plank bridge. Walk past a private chalet and over a meadow. Pass a memorial shrine on the left, then turn right on the main track, heading south up the valley. Turn off to the right along a marked path rising uphill through woodland to arrive at the hut in a small clearing.

From the Krnica Hut take the path eastwards, slightly downhill at first, and pass a sign indicating 'Špik 4 hrs'. After crossing the dry river bed, turn left at a large boulder and over a scree slope. The path rises northeastwards, then swings left in a rising traverse, and steeply round and up the nose of Gamsova Špica (1931m.) then continues steeply up a broad ridge to the peak of Lipnica (2418m.). Descend a rocky ridge to a saddle, then up a short ridge scramble to the summit of Špik.

The direct descent westwards to the valley is a challengingly execrable route of steep loose stones and boulders: it is briefly described here but a return by the ascent route may be judiciously preferred.

Return from the summit to the saddle. Descend the long scree slope north-westwards below a rock wall, then swing left to cross a field of large boulders. There follows a long steep bouldery descent through woodland to the main track leading from Krnica to Kranjska Gora.

Note

(1) Špik is the only one of a cluster of sharp rock peaks which has a marked route. There are complex tottering ridges and deep remote hollows requiring climbing skills and equipment, and best explored with a mountain guide.

(2) The map shows a minor unmarked path running roughly parallel with the main track and road northwards to Kranjska Gora from Krnica. It leaves the main track about 200m north of the torrent bed crossing, but the junction is not clear. It forms an alternative route most of the way from Krnica. The path is mainly well made, and in fact used by local shepherds, but it is narrow and difficult to follow in places. (I borrowed secateurs to cut back encroaching twigs.) At the south end, a tiny chalet may be seen in the trees above the main track. Start behind the chalet and hold a contouring course, difficult where the path crosses wash-outs; it also crosses some beautiful little ravines. At the north end bear off left through a patch of gently sloping open scrub to the end of a forestry road which comes out at Jasna.

7. KRIŠKI PODI

This plateau of naked fissured limestone, ringed by mountains, stands at the hub of the north Julians at around 2000-2300m. elevation. It is scooped into from the north by the deep craggy bay formed by the head of the Krnica valley; and from the south-west rim, great crags fall to the Zadnjica Trenta valley. The main route described here crosses Kriški podi between these two crags.

(1) THE TRAVERSE FROM KRNICA TO TRENTA

(Sketch map: Kriški podi)

Krnica Hut	1112m.
Foot of Kriška stena	1950m.
Crest of Kriška stena	2289m
Bovška vratica	2375m.
Pogačnikov dom	2052m.
Trenta	620m.
Total ascent from Krnica Hut	1263m.
Total descent to Trenta	1755m.

Time from Mihov dom to Pogačnikov dom 5-6 hours
Time from Pogačnikov dom to Trenta   3-4 hours

Start by walking to the Krnica Hut either from Kranjska Gora, or from Mihov dom (45 min.) having taken the Vršič bus from the bus station at Kranjska Gora or from the stop outside Hotel Lek. (See Route 6 above).

From the Krnica Hut, take the marked path continuing southwards up the valley, steadily rising through woodland and then scrub. At an open area of boulders and scree, be careful to turn off right at the waymarks through pine bushes and continue through bushes and scree, keeping to right of the main torrent bed, only crossing it just before a rock wall: the path continuing on the other side of the torrent bed is only clear when you reach it!

The path now rises steeply up the left-hand side of a high nose, round to the right then over to left, staying on that side until the angle eases and an alpine pasture is

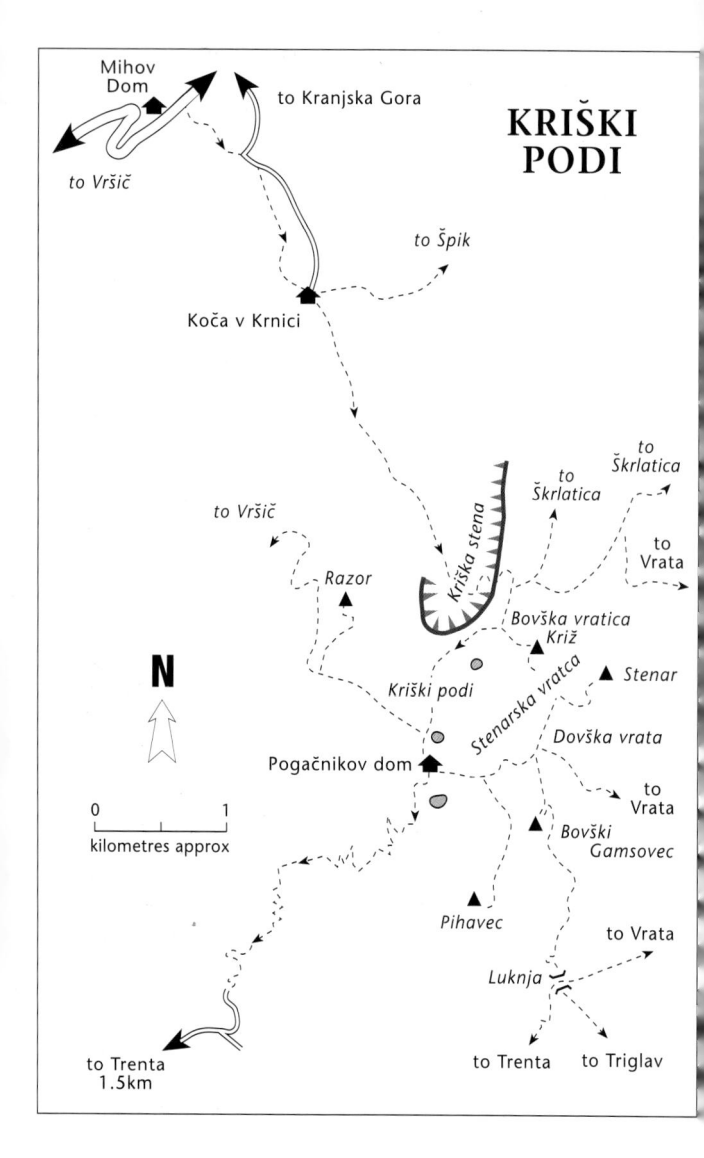

reached. Continue to the terminus of the valley in a vast bowl of scree and jumbled rocks surrounded by unbroken crags. The route, well marked, passes some huge boulders, then rises to the left up a scree slope to the foot of the crag at prominent waymarks. It is advisable to put on helmet and harness before this scree slope and well clear of the crag because it is laden with loose stones. In July 2001, there was hard snow on this slope threatening a fast slide into boulders, and an ice axe was necessary to reach the foot of the crag in safety. This snow slope was visible from the main road near the Mihov dom but hidden from the Krnici Valley until almost on arrival. However, over a number of August excursions, I have found no snow whatsoever.

Then begins the ascent of the Kriška stena rock wall, always to me a magical adventure. The route rises from the depths of the barren hollow by a scramble up easy rock, along ledges and stony terraces and up steep grooves, with sound rungs and cables wherever needed. Cushions of alpine flowers hang from cracks and tiny grooves. Great care is needed however, because of loose stones on all the ledges, and the route would be a nightmare to descend! After about 1 hour the jagged airy crest is reached. Helmet and harness can now be removed, though care is still needed, with the rock wall plunging down on one side and chasms and fissures on the other.

Close by, a path turns off eastwards to Škrlatica, Bivak IV, and Aljažev dom in the Vrata valley, providing the quickest descent in bad weather. But for the Kriški podi traverse, continue southwards along the rim of Kriška stena, rising gently on to a bare stony mound with a prominent marker post on top. For the traverse, do not turn off on the route marked for Križ, Stenar and Bovški Gamsovec, but keep close to the rim of Kriška stena and descend over short crags to a little saddle, then traverse on a good path round the side of a rocky bowl with the pool of Zgornje Kriško jezero (Upper Križ Lake), below on the left.

The route continues down through a jumbled terrain of crags, fissures and scree, and, though in clear weather the Pogačnikov Hut on its rocky knoll will be visible virtually all the way, take care to follow the paint marks as the path is not always evident in areas of bare rock and scree, and you may find your way blocked by craters and fissures.

Finally, a clear path winds across crags with the Srednje Kriško jezero (Middle Križ Lake) below on your left, and up the knoll to the hut: assured refuge with a clear safe way down to Trenta!

However, do not be deceived by the zig-zags of the descent route shown on the map into thinking it will be a stroll: the path zig-zags wildly because it descends great crags, and is quite steep. It was engineered in the First World War for mules supplying the Italian front line. The revetment walling is still intact and a wide shelf has been cut or built out, but in the upper sections much of the surface has deteriorated into loose cobbles.

The route descends past the pool of Spodnje Kriško jezero (Lower Križ Lake). The crags through which the path passes are at first bare, then clad in dwarf pine, then more and more larch and finally a forest of spruce and beech. There are fine displays of alpine flowers beside the upper sections.

As the valley is approached, the gradient gradually eases, but not greatly because the valley itself falls considerably; and it is not until the hut at the lower end of the supply cableway is reached that you arrive at a vehicular track and easy walking for the last 2 km. to the main road.

There is a bus stop at the junction, but if there is time, continue for about 500m. down the road to the next stop, where there is a bench and table. Drinks may be purchased there, or at a nearby hostelry.

(2) VARIANTS

(i) Over Razor to Vršič

About 150m. short of the Pogačnikov Hut take a clear path to the right up a steepening pasture, then a rock and scree bowl to arrive at a steep saddle at 2349m. (300m. of ascent).

A diversion from this point rises easily at first towards the summit of Razor (2601m.), a further 252m. of ascent taking about 45 minutes. The last part of this route twists up through crags but presents no difficulty.

Continuing from the saddle, the path runs almost horizontally across an easy-angled slope (snow in July 2001), then a descending traverse through crags, a zig-zag down a slope, and ramps down a steep overhung section (rungs and cables) to arrive at the stony pasture where the path traversing the flank of Prisojnik (Route 5(I)) is joined. It is still a long way to Vršič!

The total time from Pogačnikov to Vršič excluding the summit of Razor is 6-7 hours. This would be 11-13 hours from Mihov dom, but in 1993 I took just over 8 hours. Despite the high start of Vršič, I would not recommend the route in reverse because of the treacherous descent of Kriška stena. On a clear day, the descent route on Razor is fully visible from Prisojnik.

(ii) To Škrlatica and Vrata

Time: 7-8 hours from Mihov dom to the summit of Škrlatica; 4 hours from the summit down to Vrata.

From the crest of Kriška stena, turn off left on the path marked for Škrlatica, Bivak IV and Aljažev dom, taking a rough descent of about 300m. to Bivak IV (a small locked hut). From here, the path rises round rocky spurs and up a stony bowl to the rock wall on the far side near the top.

Here a plaque marks the start of a cable leading off horizontally across a rock face. It continues round spurs, across more rock faces (in one place, furnished with large hoops for footholds below the cable) and up clefts, finally landing on a broad shoulder of broken rock. (Look back and note this point well as you will need to find it on the return!) Continue across and up the broken rocks (noting the marks for return) to the summit at 2740m. This is the second highest peak in the Slovene Julians.

Return to Bivak IV at 1980m., then down a steep and bouldery path through the forest to the Aljažev dom at 1015m. in the Vrata valley. From here take a lift to the main road, where you can take the Rateče bus from the stop near the statue of Jakob Aljaž to Kranjska Gora. Failing that, you must walk the 11km. to the main road or phone by mobile or from the hut for a taxi. I always find the hut ladies very helpful.

An alternative route (which I have not done) turns left some 300-400m. after leaving the crest of Kriška stena. It loses less height (dropping only to 2,200m.) but rises over an intervening ridge at 2350m. before descending to cross the top of the scree bowl to the beginning of the equipped part of the ascent described above. (I took the lower route in 1992, not on its perceived merits but because of threatening bad weather. It arrived as I left the summit.)

(iii) Over Križ, Stenar and Bovški Gamsovec to Luknja

This variant takes in 3 peaks on the eastern perimeter of the Kriški podi plateau at the cost of some 460m. of additional ascent, and finishes at the sharp notch of Luknja, whence a descent may be made to Trenta (about 3 hours) by the spectacular First World War mule path down to the head of the Zadnjica valley, or alternatively a descent to Vrata (about 2 hours) by a steep scree path close to the foot of the North Wall of Triglav. From the crest of Kriška stena to Aljažev dom at Vrata should take 6½ - 7½ hours by this route.

From Kriška stena follow the route described above as far as the sign post on Bovška vratica. Here turn off south-eastwards for Križ. The summit at 2410m. is only 300m. away up a broad ridge with no more than 40m. of ascent.

Continuing, the path drops down the steep west side of the summit and takes a falling traverse to the broad saddle of Stenarska vratca at 2295m. I found the descent troublesome and potentially dangerous in 1997 owing to loose stones on sloping rock with a steep slope below, so take great care.

From Stenarska vratca, the summit of Stenar (2501m.) is reached by an easy route up blocky rocks. Return to the same point and continue over the stony plateau to Dovška vrata at 2178m., from where the final ridge of Bovški Gamsovec (2392m.) rises ahead. It is perfectly easy, even towards the summit, where a fine path winds past rock towers. (Indeed I remember a Slovenian family with children under 10 years of age enjoying it). To the west, the view takes in the Kriški podi plateau and the vast scree bowl rising to the great rocky peak of Pihavec (2419m.); and to east Triglav and its whole North Wall rises above and falls below.

From the rocky summit, you return a few metres and turn off down the easy south-east ridge on a good path winding down through slopes of thick turf to the deep notch of Lukjna (1758m.). Opposite, the steep craggy ridge of Plemenice rises in jagged towers in front of you. I found Bovški Gamsovec superb.

8. TRIGLAV
by the northern approaches

Introductory note

Triglav 'The Three-headed', at 2864m. is the highest of the mountains of Slovenia and is celebrated in legend, history, art, poetry and song. It is the national emblem of Slovenia.

The first recorded ascent was made on 25 August 1778 by a German surgeon and 3 local guides starting from Bohinj, where their monument stands today. In 1872, a society called 'The Friends of Triglav' was proposed, but refused by the Austrian authorities in Ljubljana who believed it would be a vehicle for national rights. The Slovenian Mountaineering Society was formed in 1883, however, and opposed commercial developments sought by the German-Austrian Alpinistic Association.

Enter Jakob Aljaž (1845-1927). He was a priest, composer, choirmaster, mountain guide and enthusiastic mountaineer. He became parish priest of Dovje, Mojstrana in 1889, a year after German mountaineers built what is now the Staničev Hut (see 'Slovenian Practicalities' 6(15)) from which the summit of Triglav is accessible. The Germans aimed to build a massive viewpoint on the summit of Triglav and a cog railway up from Bohinj. Aljaž defeated this by himself purchasing the summit area from the commune of Mojstrana. (How often have we in Scotland found conservation ownership to be the only secure way of protecting our mountain heritage from violation!)

In 1893 a message was left on top "Oh, you mountain of mountains, unite Slavic peoples!" On 31 May 1944, in winter conditions, a group of partizans ascended to unfurl the Slovenian partizan flag and proclaim the liberation of Triglav. In the summit book which had miraculously survived the War, they wrote under "Where are you from?" - "From the bushes", and under "Where are you going?" - "Into new dawns". Their commanding officer also wrote the following verse:

"Greetings, prince of mountains!
In the days we rip off our fetters
I come to your altar
To fly the banner of a new age."

TRIGLAV Northern Approaches

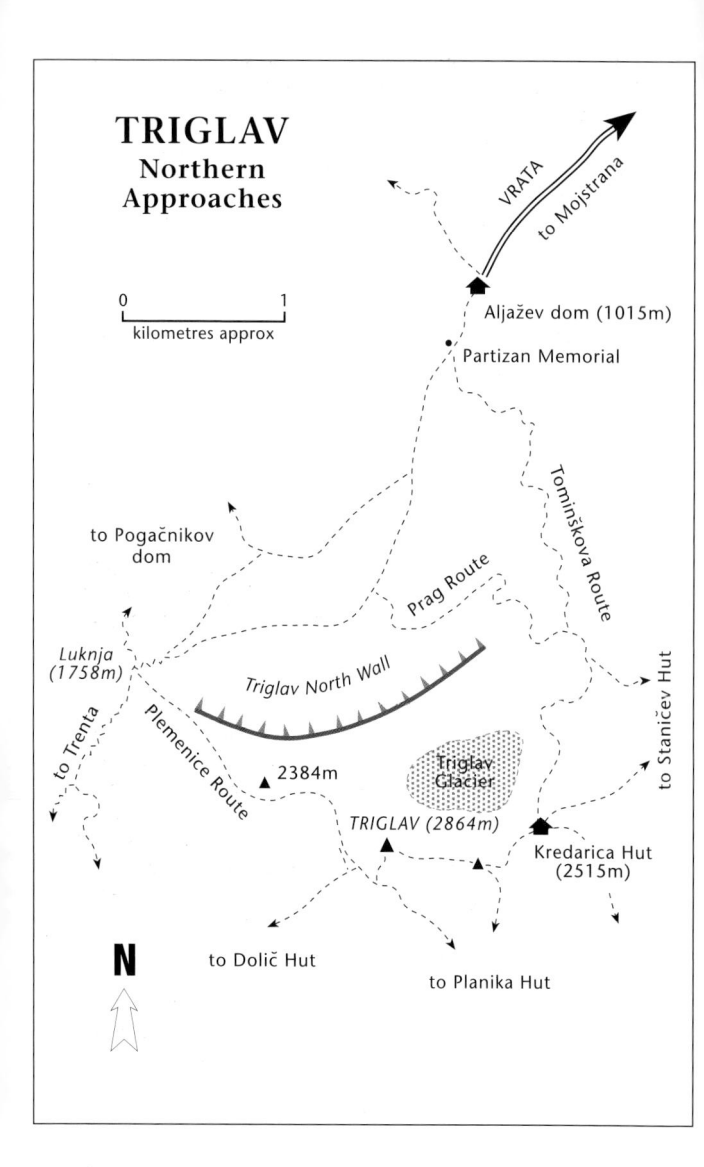

On 2 August 1944, another group ascended to excavate and hurl down the marker post of the Third Reich, and in October 1944 a third group ascended to proclaim the liberation of Belgrade.

On 25 June 1991 (the day that Slovenia declared independence from Yugoslavia), a group of Slovenian mountaineers unfurled the Slovenian flag on the summit of Triglav.

Every Slovenian aspires to climb Triglav at least once, so I suppose that others who achieve the ascent may claim to be honorary citizens.

(The foregoing historical information is mostly gleaned from a more detailed account in the Pocket Guide 'Bohinj and Triglav' published by "Turistkomerc", Zagreb, 1985.)

General description of the Northern Approaches

(Sketch map: Triglav - Northern Approaches)

Routes from east, south and west tend to be long; those from the north, steep and dramatic; but all end in 'hands-on' scrambling to the summit. The routes from every direction are described in 'How to Climb Triglav' published by Planinska Zalozba in 1991 and available locally. I shall here concentrate on the Northern Approaches.

From Aljažev dom at Vrata, or better still from the Partizan Memorial ¾ km. nearer, the Triglav North Wall may be viewed in all its splendour, one of the greatest in the Eastern Alps. (maximum height approx. 1000m.) It is the locus of many classic rock climbs. The wall is seamed across by successive strata and gashed vertically into ragged pillars. The Slovene Route near the east end is easy as rock climbs go, but if you are a rock climber, beware! - route finding is difficult, harder variants abound, and loose rock predominates.

There are 3 fine equipped routes: the Prag Route immediately left (east) of the North Wall is the easiest; the Tominškova, further left is harder, but well secured; and the Plemenice, immediately west of the North Wall, is the hardest. It starts from the Lukjna saddle very steeply and continues with free scrambling near the top. (Because of this I would not recommend the route for descent.)

From the top of either the Prag or the Tominškova Route, you must ascend through a desert of jagged limestone to the Kredarica Hut and continue up the East Ridge over Mali (Little) Triglav. From the top of the Plemenice Route you take a shorter crossing of a similar limestone desert passing on the west side of the summit pyramid to a notch in the South Ridge which is then ascended.

(1) THE PLEMENICE ROUTE AND THE SOUTH RIDGE TO THE SUMMIT

Total ascent from Aljažev dom to the summit: 1849m.
Time 5-7 hours

From Aljažev dom (1015m.) continue up the floor of the valley on a broad stony path with the stream on your left, passing the Partizan Memorial. At 2km. from the hut the Prag Route swings off left over the stream and you continue, trending right and up a steepening stony slope close to the foot of the North Wall. The path is steep and loose near the top. There is a risk from stonefall, particularly in Spring and early Summer, and in places closest to the Wall. I understand that the larger avalanche debris is cleared every Spring.

The deep sharp notch of Lukjna (1758m.) is reached suddenly. The ridge of Plemenice springs immediately up left from the saddle, sharp and steep for 600m., with pinnacles like the Aonach Eagach stacked one above the other. Intermittent cables run up slabs and grooves, and pegs stick out round airy corners. The drop down to Trenta on the right becomes steep, the drop to left down the North Wall, nearly vertical. The cables cease after the steepest part, and the marked route continues by ledge paths and slabs with large holds. I remember lifting myself up the nose of a tower on big jugs, with paint marks to confirm that this is indeed the way. The whole route is on beautiful clean rock. As the slope eases, you emerge into a 'moonscape' of jagged rocks and craters with occasional cairns helping to mark the way, which converges with the west flank of the summit to join the main route for Triglav from the Dolič Hut and approach the deep notch (Triglavska škrbina, 2659m.) affording access to the South Ridge. The crest of the notch is gained by an ascending traverse of the wall on its north side secured with pegs. (I had difficulty here on 31 August 1995 with recently fallen but frozen snow, having no ice-axe or crampons with me.)

Turning up from the notch, the broad ridge is steep, but stepped and well-secured with pegs and cables wherever needed so there is no difficulty. Then the gradient eases and you find yourself on the summit of Triglav beside the Aljažev turret. (See note.)

Note: Aljažev stolp

This is a cylindrical steel turret 2m. high with a conical roof standing on the summit of Triglav and providing a tiny refuge. It was forged for Jakob Aljaž and fixed here in 1895. Aljaž left a book here in which he wrote in Latin "Greetings traveller! Please write your name and a thought in this book. This turret and viewpoint I erected according to my own design, at my own expense and on my own land for the general good."

(2) THE PRAG ROUTE AND THE EAST RIDGE TO THE SUMMIT

Ascent from Aljažev dom to Kredarica Hut: 1500m.
Time: 5½ hours.
From Kredarica to the summit: 349m.; time 1 hour.

From Aljažev dom (1015m.) continue up the floor of the valley by a broad stony path with the stream on your left as for the Plemenice Route, passing the Partizan Memorial. At 2km. from the hut, turn left across the stream and ascend towards the foot of the great rock wall, trending left, with the assistance of pegs up minor outcrops of rock. Then take a long traverse left on ledge paths and climb more steeply up, finally up the left rim of a little stony gully to the foot of a prominent rock wall. (I remember this gully painfully as I tripped and fell into it on the descent: never lose concentration, even on easier ground until you are truly down!)

This rock wall, some 20m. high, is the Prag (or 'threshold') itself. The route climbs straight up it close against an overhang on the left, and is copiously provided with rungs, cables and cut steps. Be careful of seepage down the rock. At the top, a ledge path rises to right, and the route continues zig-zagging up with one easy secured section, then eases out into a vast area of bouldery scree, where it trends left to a great rock wall and joins the top of the Tominškova Route, which rises to left along a ledge before beginning its dramatic descent.

A few metres further, the path divides. To the left approx. 600m. away and 150m. higher, is the Staničev Hut. (See 'Deviations from the Staničev Hut')

Continuing to the right is the direct route to the Kredarica Hut and Triglav. The route crosses a desert of bare limestone with chasms, crags and fissures where care is needed to follow the marks. Finally it rises up rocky outcrops equipped with pegs and cables, to the Kredarica ridge on which stands the very large hut officially known as Triglavski dom na Kredarica, at 2515m. The original hut was opened in 1896 on land belonging to Jakob Aljaž, to great celebration attended by mountaineering clubs from several nations, and a mountaineers' choir sang 'Triglav' written and composed by Jakob Aljaž. There is a meteorological station here issuing daily reports - it may be useful to check by phone on late or early snow which might affect your plans.

The hut has 126 beds, but it is as well to check in advance at weekends and holidays because this hut is intensely popular for the final 'assault' on the summit!

Above the Kredarica Hut, the broad base of the east ridge rises steeply. Follow the well-marked path from the hut down across a shallow scree saddle and up to the bottom right hand corner of the rock face.

From this point, a continuous line of pegs rises upwards and leftwards across the face, to emerge on the narrow crest rising steeply to the subsidiary peak of Mali Triglav (2725m.). The initial section has no cables, only pegs. Footholds and handholds in the rock are plentiful but polished in places and slippery when damp. Descending with great caution in a snowstorm on 31 August, 1995 I found the snow treacherously compressed by previous climbers, and with more snow pouring like sugar off the slabs, the pegs seemed far apart! On a fine summer's day, particularly at weekends, the route carries many people, some of them clumsy, so beware of falling stones.

From the summit of Mali Triglav a fine ridge drops and then rises to the summit of Triglav, with very adequate protection, indeed, there is a cable handrail on stanchions along the narrowest section, and holds have been cut out of the rock in places - but the situation is spectacular!

See previous section for a note on the Aljažev Turret which stands on the summit.

Celebrations are in order, but you must descend! In bad weather the safest way off would be down the South Ridge (see previous section) and then south-eastwards to the Planika Hut, or westwards to the Dolič Hut.

(3) THE TOMINŠKOVA ROUTE

Ascent from Aljažev dom to Kredarica Hut: 1500m. Time: 5 hours.

This route is spectacular in its upper sections and well secured, but I found the lower section through the forest bouldery and tedious in descent. In a season of late snow, vital passages near the top may be blocked by steep hard snow banks. The Tominškova Route was engineered in 1903 by Slovenian mountaineers led by Dr. Fran Tominšek, President of the Slovenian Mountaineering Society.

Take the broad stony path up the valley floor from Aljažev dom for about 400m. to the Partizan Memorial. Here, turn left across the stream or torrent bed, and follow a steepening rightward-trending path through beech woods, crossing a timber extraction line (do not go up it!) to reach a steep torrent bed of huge boulders. Cross this and climb out to right up a continuously steep and slippery path to a rock prow where the woodland becomes thinner. Continue up rocky steps through open woodland to a short rightward traverse, then up to the right through dwarf pine and across the head of a ravine. Then up again through pine bushes, traverse right (cable) and wind up on solid bedrock through pine bushes and scattered larch.

Continue to the left hand side of a great jutting crag crowned with larch trees; and up the side by a steep zig-zag path, part scree and part rock steps, to reach a sharp saddle where the crown of the crag abuts the main rock wall. Here, put on helmet and harness!

Thence, a delightful airy climb, by rightward traverses and diagonals, often with steps cut into rock slab, with a cable alongside on the side wall. There is a slightly awkward little descent from a crest where some blocks have fallen out, followed by a gully crossing, The route continues on scree paths and through thickets of dwarf pine, and finishes with a slightly descending ledge to join the Prag Route under a great rock wall.

(4) DEVIATIONS FROM THE STANIČEV HUT

The Staničev Hut (2332m.) can be used for the ascent of Triglav, by taking an easy path to Kredarica (1 hour to the hut with 183m. of ascent, but Staničev is ½ hour nearer Vrata). There is a long tedious descent, on stony paths with some awkward little rock steps, north-eastwards by the Kot Valley to Mojstrana (3-4 hours to the roadhead).

Three ridges are accessible from the Staničev Hut:-

(1) To Cmir (2393m.)
(2) Over Visoka Vrbanova špica (2408m.) and Spodnjo Vrbanova špica (2299m.)
(3) To Rjavina (2532m.)

I understand that much of the route to Cmir (2 hours) comprises unpleasant scree ledges below the crest of the ridge.

From the map it appears that (2) and (3) would make an obvious round from the Staničev Hut, crossing the Kot valley beyond the hollow of Pekel (= Hell), but after Visoka Vrbanova špica there is a huge drop in the ridge followed by pinnacles.

Dušan Polajnar, mountain guide, advises me that the best way of doing the round would be anti-clockwise, viz from the Staničev Hut to the saddle of Dovška Vratca (2254m.), thence to the summit of Rjavina (2 hours) which is fairly easy except for a vertical 10 metre step. From the summit ridge of Rjavina, descend the steep rugged north-west face, and past Pekel to the junction of the main path down the Kot valley with the route ascending Spodjno Vrbanova špica (another 2 hours to the junction) then over Spodjno and Visoka Vrbanova špica and on more easily to the Staničev hut (another 3 hours). The whole route takes at least 7 hours in all, but the most exposed parts are equipped throughout and the very steep upper section of the descent of Rjavina is particularly well equipped.

Rjavina may of course be climbed on its own, and the following ascent is described from Pekel.

The Ascent of Rjavina (2532m) 460m. of ascent from Pekel.

Take the path labelled for Mojstrana from the Staničev Hut, down over scree and fissured limestone, to the far side of Pekel, a great cauldron-like hollow with a snow plug at the centre (about 45min.)

Here see a sign for Rjavina painted on a rock. Turn up to the right and follow a scree path to a left-rising traverse under a lumpy crag. Climb this (equipped) and continue by scree paths and steepening scrambling on shattered rock merging into a rock nose up to the foot of a great crag on the right-hand side of a ravine. Cross the foot of the ravine by an easy equipped traverse after making sure there is no-one above because it is a funnel for falling stones. Now climb up a very steep sharp arête bristling with equipment to the summit ridge of Rjavina, then turn left along the pinnacle ridge to the highest point of the mountain, by mostly easy scrambling except that there is a descent (and ascent on the return) of a 10 metre near-vertical rock wall on pegs and rungs, where self-belaying is rather more awkward than clipping on to a cable. There is a double natural window through the ridge a few metres away from the path, before gaining the summit.

From the summit ridge either-

(1) Down-climb the ascent route to Pekel, or
(2) Continue the return route along the ridge of Rjavina to the saddle of Dovjska vratca (2254m.), thence by a slanting scree path to Pekel, or
(3) From Dovjska vratca continue by an easy path to the Staničev Hut.

ENVOI

In 1992 I first stood in awe before the great North Wall of Triglav, contemplating the Slovene Route, the easiest of the rock climbing routes. I recalled to my guide how Walter Bonatti agonised before one of his daring ascents, and said that was how I felt. He answered, "But this isn't a Bonatti Route", "No, but I'm not Walter Bonatti".

The routes in this book make nowhere near the demands of a multi-pitch rock or ice climb, but they remain the stuff of dreams: some are arduous, some are airy, some are spectacular. According to personal aspirations and capacity, any of the routes may bring a sense of achievement. All are beautiful, and what more could be desired?

"May it be beautiful all around me, In beauty it is finished."
(Navaho chant.)

But remember Edward Whymper's advice "Do nothing in haste, look well to each step, and from the beginning think what may be the end".